ROME
TIME AND ETERNITY

Ezra Pound and the Pisan Cantos
(RKP, 1980)

Living in the Eternal: A Study of George Santayana
(Vanderbilt University Press, 1988)

ROME
TIME AND ETERNITY

ANTHONY   WOODWARD

IMAGES
PUBLISHING

First published in Great Britain 1995 by
Images Publishing (Malvern) Ltd.
Upton upon Severn, Worcestershire

British Library Cataloguing in Publication Data

A catalogue record for this book is available
from the British Library

ISBN 1 897817 43 6

Designed and Produced by Images Publishing (Malvern) Ltd.
Printed and Bound in Great Britain

CONTENTS

LIST OF
ILLUSTRATIONS

DEDICATION

CARISSIMAE
CONIUGI

PREFACE

To my wife, Caro, who has given so much thought and care to the content and style of this book, my debt is very great indeed, and it is dedicated to her.

Since the completion of the manuscript, the encouragement as well as selfless practical help given by Mrs Anne Turner have meant a very great deal to me.

My grateful thanks are due to the University of the Witwatersrand for a contribution to the publication expenses of this book, and in particular to Professor Brian Cheadle, Head of the Department of English, for his unstinted advice and encouragement. Dr Victor Houliston, also of the Department for English, generously checked some of my translations from the Latin texts of Fr Athanasius Kircher, S J. Monsignor Donald de Beer kindly read and corrected some sections of the book.

Mrs Janet Zambri and Miss Jill Turner, of the Inter–Library Loan Section of the University Library, were unfailingly resourceful, and I thank them. As I do also Mrs Elizabeth Adsetts, Mrs Pat Salt, and in particular Mrs Pat King, for typing the manuscript at various stages.

I am exceptionally grateful to Mr Andrew Best for his

impeccable advice and care as well as his faith in the book's possibilities.

I warmly thank the Editor of Images, Mr Tony Harold, for his enthusiasm and expert guidance, and the staff of Images for their courtesy and efficiency.

ANTHONY WOODWARD

1994

ACKNOWLEDGEMENTS

The author and publishers wish to thank the following for permission to quote from copyright material:

E.J. Brill (Leiden) for an extract from J. O'Malley: *Giles of Viterbo on Church and Reform;* Librairie José Corti, Paris, for extracts from Jean Rousset: *L'Intérieur et l'Extérieur;* Flammarion, Paris, for extracts from Yves Bonnefoy: *Rome 1630;* Gebr. Mann Verlag GmbH & Co. KG, Berlin, for an extract from Hans Kauffmann: *G.–L. Bernini, Die Figürlichen Kompositionen;* Oxford University Press for an extract from R.J.W. Evans: *The Making of the Hapsburg Monarchy;* Paulist Press (U.S.A.) for extracts from the translation by C. Luibheid contained in *Pseudo–Dionysius, The Complete Works;* Penguin Books, Ltd., for an extract from Anthony Blunt: *Borromini;* Reed Consumer Books on behalf of William Heinemann Ltd. for an extract from G. de Santillana: *The Crime of Galileo;* and Michael Joseph, Ltd., for extracts from Eleanor Clark: *Rome and a Villa.*

Every effort has been made to contact the owners of

Piranesi, Vedute di Roma, Piazza Navona

INTRODUCTION

'The Eternal City' – *Roma Aeterna* – is a phrase that softens the neon-lit glare of much travel brochure prose. It croons the enchantment of timelessness to a century more subject than any other to restlessness, mobility and change. Yet Rome itself knows its own type of subjection to time and change. It is the city of ruins as well as of churches. So: Rome of Time *and* Eternity

Ever since the 18th century, the modern world has idolised time and change. Who will deny that much of this has led to genuine progress? Rome itself is no exception. But the cheap tenements, the petrol-stations, the advertisement-hoardings, the traffic zooming through what once was the peace of the Campagna: that has not seemed like progress. For those who knew the city a hundred or more years ago it was Rome above all else in Europe which seemed to retain a beauty that was timeless: its villas, palaces and churches scattered amid gardens and along vine-clad hills which looked out over the once lonely Campagna, interspersed with graves and ruins and aqueducts –

The champaign with its endless fleece
of feathery grasses everywhere!
Silence and passion, joy and peace,
An everlasting wash of air –
Rome's ghost since her decease . . .[1]

Yet even that 19th century interlude had an element of make-believe, of post-Romantic escapism. Squalor lurking amid the picturesque; eternity conjured out of a haze of illusion; the 'Eternal City' already a tourist-trap.

Nevertheless, behind that phrase there lay a more ancient and serious claim, going back many centuries to Roman imperial times: *Roma Aeterna*. That noble pagan dream – for dream it proved to be – was baptised and incorporated into the claim of the Catholic Church that it was the inheritor of the Roman Empire, the 'Centre' of the earth. An earth which was in its turn the hub of the universe, or cosmos, still governed by the rhythms of the heavenly bodies, and reflecting, to greater or lesser extent, the radiant light of eternity. This basically pagan notion seeped into the outlook of the Christian Church. It was at odds in crucial respects with Christianity's Jewish origins: the living God of history was not quite the same thing as the eternal, unmoving One of pagan philosophers and mystics. Nevertheless, the fusion took place, and was epitomised by Catholic Rome – sacred, timeless Rome, the centre of the cosmos, the new Jerusalem.

That ideal of a Christian and Catholic *Roma Aeterna* persisted, though with considerable ups and downs, throughout the Middle

---

[1] Robert Browning, *Two in the Campagna*

18

Ages: it achieved a brief, glamorous and harmonious stability in the High Renaissance of the early 16th century; and reached a convulsive climax in the Baroque period of the 17th century. By then Protestantism had broken up the (always dubious) unity of Catholic Europe. Absolute monarchs competed for hegemony in Europe itself, as well as across the horizons of the globe that were opening out to Europe's navigators, traders and missionaries. Also, the heavens had begun to open their potentially infinite spaces to the telescope of Galileo. The old closed cosmos, enfolded in the eternal, with Rome at its centre, was bursting asunder.

It is with the 17th century period of the Baroque, and with the eternity-based ideals which previous centuries had nourished, that the earlier chapters of this book are concerned. We see its ideals of harmony, unity and light symbolised in famous monuments by the great Bernini: the Baldachin and the *Cathedra Petri* in St Peter's, so mystically Catholic and Christian, yet with such unmistakable overtones of Roman imperialism and triumphalism; the Fountain of the Four Rivers in Piazza Navona, where the continents of the globe pay homage by means of an heraldic conceit not only to a mid-17th century pope, but to the Holy Spirit. This fountain is surmounted by an obelisk whose hieroglyphs were deciphered at the time by Fr Athanasius Kircher, the most learned Jesuit of his day.

Kircher was the last figure to synthesise on a grand scale all the eclectic religious traditions of the old Europe, in the light of Eternity. There were elements of the crank as well as the scholar in Kircher. Even of the megalomaniac. Those strains of grandiosity and 'over-kill' were paralleled in the art of Bernini and his like. Such Baroque artists thought of themselves as the inheritors of classical tradition and the serene transmitters of Christian truth. Yet that restless fluidity of movement, that spectacular dynamism, that exotic floridity of the Bernini-esque Baroque were subliminal responses to new currents of time and change which were breaking the ancient moulds of European civilisation. They also hint at anguish beneath the exuberantly monumental, confident surfaces: the vertiginous spaces of Baroque vaults are crammed with figures who signal desperation as well as ecstasy. Tension and paradox abound in the Baroque of 17th century Rome. It is that great transition point when timeless ideals of a static eternity – symbolised by the consoling colossus of Michelangelo's dome of St Peter's – were in growing tension with newly emergent deities of time and change.

Thereafter the symbolism of Rome alters. We pass to works of art where time is no longer radiantly frozen in celestial space, but expands in a panorama of crumbling masonry, an endless avenue of pillared porticos, a tangled veil of vegetation, or an underground vault whose sinister chiaroschuro is dotted with tiny figures zestfully engrossed with skulls, bones and tombs. We are in the Rome of the 18th century Enlightenment, the Rome of Piranesi's engravings, which are the most famous of all images of the city, and which imaginatively foreshadow that huge expansion in the dimension of time that, like space in the previous century, both frightened and stimulated the mind of Europe. But Time Triumphant is not the whole story of Piranesi's art. He was not crushed by time. He rejoiced in what he saw, and worshipped the Romans, the men who had built those colossal structures. Then, too, the archaeologist in Piranesi happily explored the technology that buttressed the Roman defiance of time. Technology became the god of the new age of Enlightenment. Technology was Progress. Technology was Power. Thus Piranesi's Rome is a strange blend of elegy and energy – the new 'Promethean' energy that was soon to glorify time as the triumphant medium of human progress.

Hard upon Piranesi and the 18th century Enlightenment came the Revolution, Napoleon, and his dynasty-dissolving wars. The interlude of reaction after Napoleon's defeat was peppered by Liberal-nationalist insurrections, culminating in Garibaldi's occupation of Rome in 1849. The Rome of the popes, ritually still splendid and dogmatically defiant, seemed done for amid the triumphant onrush of modernity. In 1870 that new Rome of the Risorgimento established the city as capital of a united Italy, and banished the Pope to the Vatican: the Third Rome, they now called it, inspired by Mazzini's earlier vision of Italy as the greatest of nation-states, in the vanguard of the typically 19th century view of Time as Progress. D'Annunzio, Italy's foremost writer of the past hundred years – though admittedly some of his works take a bit of swallowing – echoed the forward-looking tune, and was, briefly, even a rival to Mussolini in the role of potential Duce. Ultimately, Mussolini over-reached himself. But not before his archaeologists had completed what the modernising 'developers' of Rome had begun: the destruction of that "ancient tragic peace" which 19th and early 20th century travellers from the north had cherished as a kind of aesthetic surrogate for the ideal of eternity.
Curiously enough, it was D'Annunzio also who had had some scary premonitions of what Rome was in part to become. First, an inferno of noise and banal ugliness, then the symbol of yet another kind of response to time: the Existentialist sense, deriving

21

from Heidegger, of time as Anguish and Care. The Void, *Le Néant*: that, similarly and fascinatingly, is what the modernist poet of mid-20th century Italy, Ungaretti, saw as the hidden import of the Baroque style, still so visually predominant in the city. Such, however, will not be the final word. Yves Bonnefoy, a distinguished French poet and cultural historian, saw in the Baroque style a yet deeper paradox. For him Rome is the city whose Baroque monuments at their greatest have another message. This message has little to do with semi-paganised ideals of Eternity, but much to do with time as the vehicle of Grace.

CHAPTER I

ATHANASIUS
KIRCHER

Piazza Navona! There can be few places in the world where the imagination of the restless time-traveller of the later 20th century gains such respite from its customary dispersal amid numbers and infinitude. Here is wholeness, harmony, a Centre. The continuous plashing of waters from Bernini's Fountain of the Four Rivers, the strong axial line of the obelisk surmounting its exuberant terrestrial grotto, the grand containing curve of Borromini's church of San' Agnese in Agone: all conduce to an exalting spectacle of permanence within change. The temporal flux has lost none of its ceaseless vitality. The fountains, the Roman crowds, see to that. Yet all that abounding energy is subsumed in an overarching unity by the Baroque imagination which combined intense responsiveness to the shifting reflections of light and water with a solid tectonic grasp of marble, brick and stucco. In this carnal yet sacred place we feel again that Rome is indeed *caput mundi*: holy city, world-axis, sacred mountain.

Pope Innocent X – the 'Velasquez Pope' – caused the Fountain of the Four Rivers and its crowning obelisk to be constructed under Bernini's direction at a period not long after the Jesuit order had celebrated in 1640 its first hundred years of activity. A sumptuous folio volume was issued on that occasion, *Imago Primi Saeculi*. Celebrations on its publication were organised by Cardinal Antonio Barberini, nephew of Innocent's predecessor, Urban VIII, Bernini's most famous patron. The two papal nephews, Antonio and his brother Francesco, in their own tastes and in the style of the family palace which they and their other brother, Taddeo, had built on Via Quattro Fontane, epitomise the fusion of pagan culture with Catholic devotion which had begun in the High Renaissance, had its wings clipped in the immediate post-Tridentine years of the late 16th century, and came to an exuberant climax in the Baroque courts of Urban VIII, Innocent X and Alexander VII. Of the three, Pope Urban VIII, Barberini, the friend and later the persecutor of Galileo, was the most memorable, if not the most estimable.

On the ceiling of the Gran Salone of the Barberini Palace, Pietro da Cortona had lavished spectacular virtuosity on a fresco depicting the Barberini family's special place in the designs of Providence as seen in Urban VIII's election to the papacy, thereby ensuring a link between Divine wisdom and the earthly fortunes of the Church under his guidance. On the vault graceful allegories of appropriate virtues, modelled on classical nymphs and goddesses, are like flowers of rhetoric strewn around the central devotional message. In the Baroque period, however, the Renaissance armoury of classical rhetoric was not only directed at a cultivated élite, but had broadened its appeal by making 17th century Rome the constant setting of festivals, processions and *apparati*. *Apparati* were grandiose and ephemeral structures erected in churches to frame the Holy Eucharist for Forty Hours Devotions, to illustrate a Biblical theme with all the flamboyant resources of Baroque figural art, or to raise over the coffin of some deceased dignitary a skull-begirt catafalque. In such displays all the theatrical skills of the Jesuits spoke directly to the unlettered of the invisible splendours of the divine. Ceaseless liturgical performances infused profane time with the aura of the sacred, and drew it into the orbit of the eternal. The vault-decoration of the Jesuit's most famous church, Il Gesù, depicts the Triumph of the Name of Jesus, and proclaims the defeat of Protestants and the expansion of the Church throughout the world. The other great Jesuit church in Rome, San Ignazio, tells a similar story. So too does *Imago Primi Saeculi*, the Jesuit centenary volume sponsored by Cardinal Antonio Barberini. In it there is blazoned forth the world-wide diffusion of Christianity to the four major continents of the globe through the heroic ardours of the Catholic renewal. Indeed some Jesuits of the late 16th and the 17th century shared in the millennial mood of Protestants, and identified their Order as one of the two predicted by the 12th century visionary, Joachim of Flora. Active in the world rather than contemplative or eremitic, the Jesuit Order would consummate the final stage of providential history by subduing the heretics in Europe and by taking the faith to as yet un-evangelised millions in the other three continents on Europe's expanding global horizons.

Continents were linked to the personifications of rivers – Danube, Nile, Ganges and Amazon – in the iconography of the age. On Bernini's Fountain of the Four Rivers, in Piazza Navona, all four personifications are so placed in relation to the grotto whence the waters flow that by a nicely calculated variety of *contraposto* attitudes the eye is drawn aloft by way of the papal arms to focus on the crowning obelisk. At the top of the obelisk is a dove with an olive branch in its beak, emblem of the Pamphili, the ruling papal family of Innocent X, who commissioned the monument. The dove is also the traditional symbol of the Holy Spirit. Could there be a more unfettered expression of the spiritual centrality of Rome and its ruling pontiff? The supreme high priest of Catholic Christendom draws to himself, as to a centre, the great cosmographical expansion of European civilisation and its world-redemptive religion. Here surely was an emblem of high seriousness and truth, *qualche significato vero* which, Bernini affirmed, a fountain should always proclaim.

In Rome, at the centre of the great missionary enterprises into America, Africa and Asia, which were in some degree to compensate the Church for the losses experienced in the European heartland of Christendom, there is to be found the figure of Fr Athanasius Kircher SJ, an egregious polymath. To him throughout the mid-seventeenth century the Jesuit missionaries from all four quarters of the globe sent accounts of their discoveries and vicissitudes. Their reports were important ingredients in some of the encyclopedic tomes in which Kircher synthesised the traditional learning of the Christian centuries, along with its hermetic accretions. A recent authority on the 17th century has described him as personifying "the whole Catholic reformulation of the Christian Humanist thought of the Renaissance . . . the summit of the Counter-Reformation's intellectual ambition . . . His writings form a sort of phenomenology of the occult or . . . a *Summa*

Magiae for the neo-scholastic age".[1]

Despite Kircher's fame in the 17th century, he is today in the English-speaking world for the most part pretty thoroughly forgotten, except in the most learned of journals, and in the occasional derogatory reference to his role in unravelling the hieroglyphs on Roman obelisks, among them those on the obelisk of the Four Rivers Fountain in Piazza Navona. Kircher interpreted them along the lines which Valeriano in the 15th century Renaissance had derived from Horapollo, a writer of late antiquity: as symbols of a hidden wisdom which had been transcribed in ancient Egypt by a legendary seer, Hermes Trismegistus. Kircher's learning was in most ways of that traditional type which was specially receptive to the authority of ancient sources, such as the *Corpus Hermeticum*, which had been concocted by neo-Platonists in late antiquity and purported to draw on ancient Egyptian wisdom. Casaubon had exposed the fraud in 1614 but, along with some others, Kircher ignored his findings. Kircher had the type of mind in part exemplified in an English context by Burton's *Anatomy of Melancholy*, though devoid of Burton's zany, inconsequential charm; whilst in his haphazard empiricism and selective scepticism, there was something, too, of Sir Thomas Browne. His most telling counterpart in English culture of the early 17th century, however, if you discount Kircher's Catholic orthodoxy, would be Robert Fludd, the magus and polymath who synthesised the occult hermeticism which percolated Christian culture down the centuries. Fludd had a famous clash with Mersenne, the Catholic Minim friar who was a friend of Descartes, and the ambiguous 'facilitator' of the scientific rationalism of the first part of the 17th century.

Plate 1: Engraving by C. Bloemaert for Athanasius Kircher's
Obeliscus Pamphilius *(Romae, 1650)*

*At the top left, Saturn with his scythe, a symbol of Time,
hovers malevolently over an obelisk toppled by the ages.
Nevertheless Hermes in person confirms Kircher's
interpretation of hieroglyphs by pointing to a fold–out page
of the latter's* Obeliscus Pamphilius. *Fame, clasping her
trumpet, dotingly looks on. A pile of learned tomes –
Egyptian, Chaldean, Pythagorean – is visible at left.*

Kircher's copious divagations between science and magic, magnificently illustrated by plates that blend ornate fancy with painstaking pedantry, encompassed all the Baroque passion for the gigantic, the intricate, and the exotic, along with the century's growing ardour for experimentation. Many areas of knowledge that in the 20th century are crisply separated into disciplined procedures, or dismissed out of hand as subjects for serious investigation, existed in a pell-mell of excitable omnivorousness in the early 17th century, that quintessential 'age of transition'. In prodigiously encyclopedic tomes last-ditch attempts were made by the savants of Baroque Europe to unite scattered and diverse sciences within systems microcosmically reflecting the hidden harmonies implanted by God in his creation. Sir Thomas Browne's *The Garden of Cyrus* was a scaled down example. A similar type of ambition was manifest, part playfully, in English metaphysical poetry; in the mellifluous riddling of Marino and the Marinisti; and in the more taxing contortions of the Spanish Baroque poetry of *agudeza*, where poems akin to verbal ciphers tested the devout ingenuity of a cultivated élite. It was an age fascinated by the ingenious correlation of verse and visual image in decorative emblems, by the gnomic distillations of heraldic *imprese*, and by the arcane wisdom supposedly latent in enigmatical hieroglyphs.

Along with his famously erroneous Egyptological researches, in which he was encouraged by a succession of mid-17th century Popes, Kircher engaged in scientific work on contagion theory, thermometers, lighting devices, lenses, magnets, mathematical machines and acoustics. In the cause of science he had himself lowered into Vesuvius prior to a threatened eruption in order to verify the preliminary phenomena. On a later occasion he concocted an elaborate tome assessing the miraculous credentials of the cruciform shapes which appeared on various articles of clothing in the area subsequent to an eruption. He invented a speaking-tube and installed it in the Collegio Romano between the porter's lodge and his own room, and was thus apprised beforehand of the constant stream of learned visitors and touring dilettanti who came either to consult him or to view his collection of rarities. This collection of objects from all quarters of the globe survived as the Museo Kircheriano until the late 19th century when, in a post-Risorgimento spring-cleaning, its contents were scattered among the other museums of Rome. Kircher made acoustic devices, 'artificial echoes', water-organs and many such mechanical toys for the palaces and gardens of 17th century Rome, where prodigious spectacles of ephemeral splendour were constantly being devised by both the ingenious artificers of the Roman Baroque, and artists as eminent as Bernini. Kircher's technological sleights of hand were accompanied by deeper concerns, which took him to the farther reaches of contemporary speculation on music, language, mathematics and astronomy. His book on Magnetism well illustrates the outlook: in it Kircher argued that all movement and action throughout the universe were matters of secret sympathies and attractions, with God being, so to speak, the central magnet. This situates Kircher on the animistic wing of hermetic neo-Platonism, which was experiencing a renewal among some Jesuits as well as among other religious orders in the early and mid-17th century.

It was to Kircher in Rome that the Jesuit missionaries directed their accounts of the new world's wonders which their dangerous apostolate was unfolding to them: he became a sorting-house for the dissemination of new knowledge among the learned men of Europe, who still kept open an international network of humanistic and scientific scholarship, despite the sectarian ferocities that preoccupied their rulers. Indeed it had been in order to escape the ravages of the Thirty Year's War in Germany that Kircher, after a fruitful stay with Peiresc, the great humanist scholar and virtuoso of Provence, had in 1635 eventually made his way to Rome, where he became Professor of Mathematics at the Collegio Romano. From the active duties of that post he soon retired, and with the blessing of his order and a succession of Popes he remained in Rome devoting himself thereafter to his stupendous intellectual exertions. Among them two volumes, *Prodromus Coptus sive Aegyptiacus* (1636) and *China Monumentis* (1667), exemplify the spirit in which he sifted and collated the exotic material which the Jesuit missionaries directed to him.

That spirit was one in which the passion for unity was predominant. Although the Church had accepted as a *fait accompli* the dispersal of European Christendom into autonomous nation-states, and was now fast coming to terms with the variety of non-European cultures in other parts of the globe, an ideal of apostolic universality still governed her outlook: a universality and a unity centred in Rome. Among the findings in the Far East which were brought to the attention of the Jesuits was a fragment known as the stone of Sian-Fu. On its central portion were inscribed Chinese characters describing the arrival in China of a Christian mission active in the 7th and 8th centuries. On the margins were characters that defeated the mandarins, but which were eventually identified by Jesuits in India as Siriac lettering. The stone was a commemorative trace of early Christian Nestorian missionaries who had reached China and worked there successfully for several generations. The discovery fitted Kircher's diffusionist vision which saw all cultural movements as expansion outward from a centre, and was also for him a providential sign directed at the Church as it once again moved outward on its universal mission. The Eastern Mediterranean and adjacent territories were, so to speak, the heartland whence divine Providence commenced its operations. Was not Paradise situated there? And was it not there that Noah had established his Ark, a prefigurative symbol of the Church? R.J.W. Evans, the historian of the 17th century Hapsburg monarchy – some of whose members were among Kircher's most notable patrons – has extracted the kernel of Kircher's outlook in an incisive and illuminating paragraph:

> *Immediately after the Flood, says Kircher, the Egyptian state was founded, or perhaps revived, by Cham, alias Osiris, son of Noah. A sophisticated and well-ordered polity, with a firm official religious ethos, it nevertheless faced from the outset one fundamental duality: God's revelation to men, handed from Adam to Noah, was continually perverted by those who sought to use the power it conveyed in the service, not of spiritual wholeness, but of operative magic. The greatest profaner of this true and universal faith was Cham himself; its greatest vindicator his grandson, Hermes (or Mercurius) Trismegistus, whom Kircher reveres as statesman, lawgiver, the author of the hieroglyphics. Under Hermes the battle-lines were already draw up: a learned and sagacious priesthood was forced by the devilish machinations of its enemies to veil the divine message in*

symbolic forms. Can we not already descry in this antithesis
the contours of seventeenth-century European culture too,
and its Baroque interplay of light and darkness?[2]

Cham was also the forebear of Nimrod, the founder of the Tower
of Babel, and anti-type of all that is symbolised by Noah and his
Ark. Dispersed amid a babel of tongues across the breadth of the
globe after the destruction of the tower, and deprived through sin
of the original purity of a single universal language, the scattered
peoples were now once again being drawn into the orbit of the
Church of Rome, the new ark of salvation. Unlike some of his
Jesuit colleagues, such as de Nobili in India and Martini in China,
Kircher did not have an ecumenically accommodating attitude to
the diversity of cultures. He saw the myths and rites from various
exotic parts of the earth as idolatrous parodies originating in a
basic idolatry prevalent in ancient Egypt and thereafter diffused
across the globe. Yet one element of Egyptian culture had
preserved the beneficent arcane wisdom existing prior to the
Flood, in the shape of Hermes Trismegistus, who transcribed in
sacred hieroglyphics the essentials of divine knowledge: *Sapientia,*
quae vel ipsum Moysen discipulum habuerit . . . "A wisdom which
had even Moses as disciple".[3] From Egypt it also reached the early
sages of Greece. That, so to speak, was the acceptable face of
ancient Egypt; less so its role as the centre of diffusion for
idolatries.

To modern eyes, much in Kircher's *Arca Noe* and *Turris Babel*
seems the raving of a bibliocentric bigot and crank. Yet we do
well to remember how difficult it was in the 17th century for even
a very learned man to envisage the time-scale that is now taken for

granted. Two assumptions made history conveniently apprehensible for Kircher and his contemporaries: the creation of the world only 4,053 years before the birth of Christ, and the extinction in the year 1657 BC of all but eight human beings in the Flood. The Flood in turn was a *terminus post quem* for the subsequent history of all nations, which could be pieced together from the Greek and Roman histories as well as from the Old Testament.[4] Even Vico, in the early 18th century, let us remember, shared such assumptions. He, like Kircher, wrote providential history; but Vico was to effect a radical shift. Instead of assuming that degeneration from original purity was the key to historical understanding, he foreshadowed the evolutionary attitude of a later period. Kircher, however, was predisposed otherwise. Although his ideals were under considerable strain in the Christian world of the 17th century Kircher made one of the last comprehensive attempts to synthesise a variety of geographical and historical factors within the ambit of a providential scheme. Pre-figured in the Old Testament was the New, and the church of the New Testament, the new Ark of Salvation, was a means of integrating all times and places within a synthesis pre-figured from eternity. Implicit in such an attitude is the stabilisation of contingency by means of predetermined patterns or archetypes. It is a sacralising myth of timelessness in the guise of a providential theory of historical events. The goal of history was the restitution of an aboriginal unity.

Such was the response of one learned and pious Roman Jesuit to the expanding geographical horizons of the 17th century. What of the cosmological expansion that was agitating the intellects of Europe in the wake of Copernicus' heliocentric hypothesis? Here too Kircher, in a volume entitled *Itinerarium Ecstaticum*, showed a determination to preserve ideals of unity and centredness, despite accepting many of the telescopic discoveries of Galileo: moons of Jupiter undreamt of by Ptolemy and Aristotle; more stars in the heavens; vaster distances; the moon's surface corrugated and mountainous, thus dispelling the ancient belief that the heavens were made of a pure and changeless substance distinct from the corruptible four elements of the earthly centre. In the background, too, there could not but be an awareness of the pantheistic speculations of Giordano Bruno concerning the possible infinitude of the cosmos: "Tear away the concave, the convex surfaces which restrict both within and without so many elements and heavens . . . God is glorified not in one, but countless suns; not in a single earth but in a thousand. I say, in an infinity of worlds . . . "[5] In such expressions Bruno was pushing to an extreme, in the light of Copernicus, implications latent in the theories of that extraordinary 15th century Cardinal of the Catholic Church, Nicholas of Cusa. Nicholas had relativised the notion of a centre and posited the physical universe as an *infinitas complicata*, a contraction of the true and total infinity of God. The pantheistic possibilities of Nicholas of Cusa's guarded utterances were not lost on the impetuous and enthusiastic Giordano Bruno.

The writings of Nicholas of Cusa were well known to Kircher, and he was fully abreast of all the astronomical debates of the first part of the 17th century. It has been suggested that he secretly espoused the Copernican-Galilean system, to which, however, it was neither safe nor seemly for a Jesuit openly to adhere. In his *Itinerarium Ecstaticum* he settled, as did many of his Order, for the compromise system of Tycho Brahe, where the other planets did indeed circle the sun, but the entire group of sun and planets revolved around the stable earth.

In Kircher's imaginary journey, Theodidactus, a devout enquirer after celestial knowledge, is taken on a guided tour amid the sun, the planets and the fixed stars to the boundaries of the empyrean by Cosmiel, an eloquently omniscient member of the angelic hierarchy. It is worth noting that Cosmiel is quite at ease with the notion that space is homogeneous and that there is no traditional division between the changeless substance of the heavens and the elements beneath the moon; but Kircher's homogeneous space is a magnetic field full of vital influences and mystical affinities, not the coldly quantitative mathematical space of Galileo or Descartes. His imagination was rapturously responsive to the immensity of heavenly space, in a manner at times verging on the Bruno-esque. At one point Cosmiel in a striking phrase remarks of the stars that *omnes enim ob incredibilem distantiam in nihilum abierunt* – "on account of their incredible distance they disappear into nothingness". There is nevertheless a single purpose animating this huge cosmic creation: the incarnation of the Logos for the redemption of mankind and the greater glory of God. Kircher uses the terminology of Nicholas of Cusa in his exposition of the doctrine of the Incarnation: Christ as *maximum contractum* or *concretum* unites in himself not only the various levels of created existence, as man does, but also the Godhead itself, *Maximum Absolutum*.

Kircher combined intense imaginative responsiveness to the seemingly illimitable tracts of cosmic space not just with a Christocentric doctrine but with an encompassing theocentrism as well. This emerges tellingly in one of the concluding chapters of the *Itinerarium* entitled 'De Coelo Empyreo'. Cosmiel, having conceded that the Empyrean, the abode of God and the blessed, must be made of an infinitely subtler and rarer matter than the rest of the universe, represses further speculation on the part of Theodidactus, simply affirming that all the vast spaces through which he and his pupil have travelled *comparatione ad coelum empyreum facta, non nisi punctum censeri debere* – "when compared with the empyrean must be deemed but a point".[6] Then, with a rhetorical expansion comparable to the opening out of some vista on a Baroque vault like that of the Gesù or San Ignazio, where graciousness and exaltation mingle in a celestial luminosity, Cosmiel invokes a vision of the Court of Heaven, thereby rounding off the dimensions of the universe and harmonising them into an ultimate unity satisfying to the religious imagination. The inwardness of faith, at this 17th century transitional phase, could still be externalised by traditional iconographical emblems, which indeed are riotously abundant in Baroque vaults and religious painting, possibly lending weight to Georges Poulet's insight that "in the furious deployment of forms which constitutes the most evident trait of Baroque art one must observe less a sign of the conquest of space by the mind, than of the impossibility for the mind finally to accomplish this conquest".[7] Something of that Baroque over-kill emerges in the Kircher passage on the celestial court of the Empyrean:

> . . . *Where the whole council-chamber of the heavenly king and the transcendent court with its varied ranks of Elders, ranged as it were in choirs, will resound through all eternity not with three, four or five but with an*

unimaginable symphony of voices of surpassing excellence.
There the chorus of Virgins, together with the choruses of
Confessors, mingling their voices with the choirs of Martyrs,
Apostles and Patriarchs, all sounding in harmony together
with the triple orders of Angels, refreshing themselves
eternally at the spring of the water of eternal life, will, with
ceaseless exultation, attune that eternal Alleluia to God, the
supreme choirmaster as it were, directing His intellectual
symphony, while His breath gives life to the organ of His
own mouth. There, following the Lamb of God, the organ
and music of that eternal dwelling-place, they will sing a
new and admired song: that epithalamium and wedding
song of the marriage of the Word of God with human
nature in the womb of the immaculate Virgin. There the
remembrance of the labours and torments suffered on this
earth for the love of God – a certain dissonance, as it were,
combined and intermingled with the chords of eternal, most
blissful life – will dissolve into the sweetness and most
perfect harmony of all things.[8]

Immersed in the ever-renewing waves of such rhetoric we may
find ourselves reminded of sentences in which Leibniz makes
explicit what is surely implied by Kircher, and which perhaps give
to the remarks of Poulet a more positive turn. Leibniz writes of
"the blessed, by a continuous growth into the infinite, once
admitted into God, that is into the universal harmony . . . and
having embraced it as it were by a concentrated stroke of vision,
possess it too as perpetually renewed; for by the differing
contemplation of the parts of joy they infinitise its delight, since

thought, just like pleasure, is nothing without perpetual renewal and progress".[9] Leibniz here surely crystallises an important feature of Baroque sensibility, despite its never having quite lost the sense of an encompassing harmony. Freedom and expansiveness, which are as much a part of the Baroque as the faith in ultimate harmony, are reflected in the increased plasticity of sculpture as well as painting; in the breaking down of barriers between spectator and work of art; in the fusion of media; in melting, blending sinuosity; but most of all perhaps in the prominence of vast spaces, which can plausibly be held to reflect an awareness of new cosmological dimensions. We find such awareness in another Jesuit famous in his time, Daniele Bartoli, who like Kircher responded to the missionary expansion in the East as well as to the new cosmology: the vastness and beauty of the created universe are hailed with devout enthusiasm in Bartoli's writings and find appropriate support in sections of the Book of Job. As De Santillana remarked in *The Crime of Galileo*, even the great scientist "knew the Jesuits as modern-minded humanists, friends of science and discovery. Those he feared were the professors".[10] The new cosmology did not necessarily in the 17th century cause a sense of intellectual frustration, such as we find in Donne's *Second Anniversary*, let alone Pascal's far more drastic *Le silence de ces espaces infinis m'effraie* (The silence of those infinite spaces terrifies me) – which, incidentally was not Pascal's own view, but that of an imaginary atheistical interlocutor.

Indeed many men could be, like Kircher, rapturously responsive to divine magnitude and power as mirrored in the creation; they could accept the homogeneity of space, in which, however illogically, the traditional image of upward and ascending movement to the transcendent remained in place. A painting by Cigoli, the friend of Galileo, in Santa Maria Maggiore in Rome, catches something of the paradoxicality of the age: Mary, Queen of Heaven, stands in traditional fashion on the moon, but a moon which revealed mountains and craters as they appeared through Galileo's telescope, with all the concomitant suggestions of a changed and enlarged cosmic space which the cultivated members of that intensely religious culture of the first half of the 17th century would instantly have recognised. As Murray Roston puts it, "The Church did not so much absorb the New Philosophy as enormously enlarge its own conceptions to include the infinite that had been revealed to it".[11] A certain insouciance, based on firm inner faith in the sacred mysteries of religion could – as for instance in Milton's *Paradise Lost* – allude to the new theories, but as a matter of conscious artistic choice retain much of the old cosmology as suitable to the epic story. We should remember that heliocentrism, even at the mid-17th century, could still be regarded as one hypothesis among others, and though the modern mind "finds it repugnant to admit the co-existence in one and the same discourse of two contradictory theories which seem mutually exclusive, the period seems to have no such difficulty: examples abound."[12]

Support for the view expressed in that passage could be found by considering the strategies of Marino, the epitome in his intricately ravishing bravura of much that we mean by the southern Baroque temperament. The lubricity of some of his verses offended the pious, especially in *Adone*. In that poem there is also a substantial section lauding the discoveries of Galileo and his telescope. Marino was, however, infinitely adaptable, like most men of letters of his age, and in one of three Sacred Discourses delivered to the court of Turin during the first quarter of the 17th century, he refers with calm interest in the course of *De Cielo* to physical speculations on the heavens, but affirms that for his part he is content for the heavens still to represent the *Cielo Religioso*[13]: "The baroque poet, at the very same time as celebrating the newly appeared marvels of the sky due to the telescope, does not forget . . . that the sky is also a habitation . . . a habitation, or rather a temple. For if the temple is to be a symbol and figure of the cosmos, it is, inversely, the cosmos which is a temple, ordained for celebrating the glory of God."[14]

It is just such an image of the heavens as a habitation and temple that we find in *La Divina Sapienza*, one of the most famous frescoes of the 1630's, albeit by a painter, Andrea Sacchi, of classicising not baroque tendency. In the centre of the ceiling of a room adjacent to the chapel in the Barberini Palace in Rome, Divine Wisdom, a celestial female figure, is seated on a lion-headed throne, attended by a group of allegorical virtues originating in the Old Testament's Book of Wisdom and Book of Proverbs. The figure of Divine Wisdom has a sun, a Barberini heraldic device but also a long-standing symbol of the divine, emblazoned on her bosom. The sun thus prominently centred, with the earth as prominently placed to one side, may conceivably recall the theories of Copernicus and Galileo currently being bandied about.[15]

This prominence of the sun has led one writer [16] to surmise that Sacchi's *Divina Sapienza* fresco was composed under the inspiration of Tomaso Campanella, author of one of the most famous utopian schemes of the Renaissance and Baroque periods, *The City of the Sun*; in doctrine part naturalistic, part neo-Platonic. Campanella, like Giordano Bruno, was a renegade Dominican. Despite having experienced over twenty years of imprisonment, first in Naples by the Spaniards and then more briefly by the Roman Inquisition, Campanella enjoyed after his release a brief spell of favour at the court of Urban VIII, for whom he even drew up a horoscope, since the Pope had been perturbed by astrological predictions of his own death. In one of Campanella's writings, *Discorsi ai Principi di Italia*, he proposed the establishment of a world-monarchy in which the Pope would be the sacrosanct supreme ruler of a harmonised world-order. The rather attractive idea, backed by some suggestive circumstantial evidence, that Campanella's views were the inspiration of Sacchi's *La Divina Sapienza* fresco seems, alas, to be implausible; even Urban VIII's fear of death would hardly persuade him to sanction, as formulator of such a central iconographical statement, the heterodox thinker and maverick priest, Campanella.

More pertinent is the use made by Panofsky of an incident associated with Sacchi's *La Divina Sapienza*. He draws on a passage in Tetius's *Aedes Barberinae*, an encomiastic contemporary volume celebrating the then newly constructed glories of the Barberini Palace. He quotes the incident from Tetius in the course of his essay on 'Symbolic Images'[17], when discussing the importance of Christian neo-Platonism in the iconographical tradition of European art, and in particular those moments of vision when an eternal archetype is manifest in a concrete temporal incident. The world, in a Christian neo-Platonist perspective, is full of images and reflections of God, so that we see the divine shining forth through the temporal and have fleeting intuition of the harmonious unity that underlies all multiplicity. In the incident to which Panofsky refers, Tetius saw the majesty and wisdom of God crystallised in the figure of Urban VIII who, quite by accident, had sat at table under the Sacchi fresco when a text on Divine Wisdom was chosen for the lesson. The Pope is like a reflection of God the Son, the Logos, since in patristic theology the personified Wisdom of the Old Testament was a prefiguration of the higher wisdom which was God the Son, as revealed in the doctrine of the Trinity. The Jerusalem Bible comments on the overtones of Greek philosophy in the passage of the Old Testament concerning Divine Wisdom, which was later to be fused with the Johannine doctrine of the Logos. That fact, taken in conjunction with Panofsky's comments on the neo-Platonic background of the incident in Tetius, reminds us that elements of the philosophical theology of late antiquity were incorporated into Christianity in the early centuries of the faith, thus grafting onto the specifically Christian revelation late antiquity's ideal of cosmic unity, and of a harmony that subsumed time within the eternal.

Three Roman visual images – the Fountain of the Four Rivers with its obelisk, and the Baldachin and *Cathedra Petri* in St Peter's – will at the climax of each of the two chapters that follow draw out some of the implications of that moment in the Barberini Palace.

Notes to Chapter 1

1. R.J.W. Evans, *The Making of the Hapsburg Monarchy,* (OUP, 1979) 440-1

2. Evans, op. cit., 436

3. A. Kircher, *Oedipus Aegyptiacus III* (1) (Romae, 1652-4))

4. cf. J. Godwin, *Athanasius Kircher* (Thames and Hudson Ltd., 1979) 23. The only widely accessible modern account in English. Good, but brief text. Abundant illustrations. Two substantial and fascinating accounts of Kircher exist in Italian: D. Pastine, *La Nascita dell'Idolatria* (Firenze, 1978) and V. Rivosecchi, *Esotismo a Roma Barocca: Studi Sul Padre Kircher* (Roma, 1982). I have not managed to obtain Thomas Leinkauf's *Mundus Combinatus: Studien zur Struktur der barocken Universalwissenschaft am Beispiel Athanasius Kirchers SJ* (Berlin, 1993)

5. ed. D.S. Robinson, *Anthology of Modern Philosophy* (New York, 1931) 50

6. A. Kircher, *Iter Ecstaticum Coeleste* (Nuremberg, 1660) 363 . . . 431. [This is the second edition of the *Itinerarium Ecstaticum* published in Rome in 1656.]

7. G. Poulet, *The Metamorphoses of the Circle* (Johns Hopkins Press, 1966) 15

8. Kircher, Iter., 432

9. G.W. Leibniz, *Confessio Philosophi*, (Frankfurt-am-Main, 1967) 100

10. G. de Santillana, *The Crime of Galileo* (Heinemann, 1958) 8

11. M. Roston, *Milton and the Baroque* (Macmillan, 1980) 14

12. D. Souiller, *La Littérature Baroque en Europe.* (Presses Universitaires de France, 1988) 43

13. G.B. Marino, *Dicerie Sacre e la Strage degl'Innocenti*, a cura di G. Pozzi (Turin, Einaudi, 1960): III, 'Il Cielo', 402

14. P.-H. Michel, 'La Querelle du Géocentrisme'. *Studi Secenteschi* (2) 1961, 117

15. A.S. Harris, *Andrea Sacchi* (Princeton University Press, 1977) 12

16. G.S. Lechner, 'Tommaso Campanella and Andrea Sacchi's Fresco of Divina Sapienza in the Palazzo Barberini' *The Art Bulletin*, Volume LVIII (1) 1976

17. E. Panofsky, *Symbolic Images*, (Phaidon, 1978) 156-7, cf. as well, Marc Fumaroli, *L'Age d'Eloquence* (Droz, 1980) 204-209

CHAPTER II

THE
COSMIC
ICON

"The Christian world of the Middle Ages is still that of the Greek cosmos, enriched but not overthrown."[1] Those words of a great scholar refer to the neo-Platonic, cosmological version of Christianity which was to be found with varying degrees of emphasis not only throughout much of the Middle Ages, but which, amplified in the Renaissance by hermetic doctrines, persisted into the Baroque period, and found its extravagant climax in the writings of Athanasius Kircher. Kircher's writings are full of passages which exemplify the prevalence in hermetic, neo-Platonised Christianity of factors such as unity, harmony and light. They were frequently accompanied down the centuries by the image of a circular egress and return to a central and transcendent divine principle of unity. The triple formula of harmony, unity and light gave priority to the eternal over the temporal, although time was not thereby tendered nugatory. This can be seen from Plato's *Timaeus*, the source of so many of the ideas we are considering, where time is described as the moving image of the eternal. This was primarily on account of the regular circular movement of the celestial bodies, which in turn were seen to impart regularity to the material realm. Thus time was a principle of order and, as it were, "the graduated ring of an outer circle revolving around the inner wholeness which is eternity itself".[2] It is clear how easily such Greek notions could be adapted to Christianity. Temporal created being, whose final cause was God, was constantly being assimilated to the eternal by participation in the divine Ideas contained in the Logos. Four quotations from Kircher's works will set us on our path:

> In the unity of the Monad we behold the undivided Mind and Divine essence as productive of all things . . . The first unity is as it were the exemplar of all things, preceding all multiplicity, and consequently preceding all otherness, oppositeness, inequality and division; and although a unity of this kind is neither dual, nor triple, nor quadruple, it is all those things which are dual, triple quadruple, etc. If species are distinguished numerically, this absolute unity is certainly of no species, nor has it name or figure – but it is all in all things.[3]
>
> God, best and greatest, showed us the admirable harmony of the heavenly bodies . . . the harmonies of inferior things are nothing but echoes of the lofty notes of the heavens, reverberating in this inferior world in accordance with their nature . . . The ancient Egyptians . . . observed the sympathy, agreement, and relationships that sublunary things have with one another, and those that connect the manifest world with occult forces.

Plate 2: Athanasius
    Kircher, Musurgia
    Universalis,
    Frontispiece
    (Romae, 1650)

The harmony that encompasses and pervades the cosmos is indicated by the terrestrial globe encircled by some of the symbols of the zodiac, and surmounted by the allegorical figure of Musica; she clasps with one hand the lyre of Apollo, and with the other the pan-pipes of Marsyas. This cosmological 'Musica' is irradiated by beams from the triangle at the top, symbolising the Trinity, whose radiance in its turn is encircled by the nine angelic choirs. Below, in the left-hand corner, Pythagoras, the legendary founder of musical theory and proponent of numerical harmonies as the key to the Musurgia Universalis, points with his left hand toward hammering blacksmiths who, in legend, revealed to him the relation of weight and tone. One of the nine Muses, Polyhymnia, begirt by a battery of musical instruments, confirms the centrality of music as a key symbol of cosmic harmony.

*They founded a sacred and mystical philosophy in which
these matters were given out under various symbols
designed to veil them, called hieroglyphs; and it is this
science, lost to our day, which we will restore by God's
grace in Oedipus Aegyptiacus.*[4]

*God is the father of lights, in whom there is no change, nor
shadow of change. He is the father of lights, in whom are
no shades; the fountain and source of all light; all things
which are on earth are appearances, as it were reflections
of the one God, who, though single, cannot but appear as
varied manifestations in his creatures, as light is in the
colours of opaque bodies . . . For God, supremely good, is
infinite goodness in act, and from the nature of the
goodness it wishes to communicate, it diffuses from within
itself varied lights which Saint Dionysius (the Areopagite)
calls theophanies . . .*[5]

*For whoever sees the light of the moon sees the light of the
sun which is indistinguishable form the light of the moon,
since the light of the moon is no other than the reflection of
the sun's light on us. So therefore whoever sees the
wisdom, providence and love of God shining in this world,
also sees God – so Saint Dionysius (the Areopagite) bears
witness: all created things being no other than mirrors or as
it were rays of the divine wisdom reflected to us . . . But let
us hear the opinion of the inspired Plotinus on these things,
in his Third book concerning the three divine hypostases.*[6]

Plate 3:   *Athanasius Kircher,*
           Ars Magna Lucis
           et Umbrae,
           Frontispiece
           (Romae, 1671)

Physical light, as a metaphor for degrees of intellectual and spiritual enlightenment, is variously symbolised by this plate. At the very top is the Tetragrammaton, the Hebrew lettering for the ineffable name of God. Apollo, the sun–deity, a Christianised avatar of the Godhead, is radiantly lit; above his head the finger of God points to the Bible as highest source of illumination; a beam runs, diagonally from top left downwards, to pierce and illuminate a Platonic cave. To the right of the Hebraic lettering symbolising God at the top, is the hand of Reason, conjoined to an "inner eye". Reason, or Ratio, *is a mediated knowledge inferior to the direct Biblical illumination; and hence the more shadowy figure of the moon–goddess is depicted beneath. The senses, near the bottom, to the right, are aided by a telescope. To the left, profane knowledge is paid a grudging tribute by the symbol of a covered candle dimly illuminating a book.*

Let us now unpack some of the implications of these quotations, first by tracing them to their source in the neo-Platonism of late antiquity and in the mystical theology of early Christianity, then by following some of their vicissitudes down the centuries until they bring us back to that Baroque 17th century polymath, Athanasius Kircher, whose writings synthesise for the last time so much of traditional Christian neo-Platonism and its hermetic accretions.

At the end of the last passage quoted, Kircher goes on to expound a section of the *Enneads* of Plotinus. Plotinus, who wrote in the Third Century AD and had considerable influence on the neo-Platonising element in St Augustine, was, like so many thinkers of antiquity and of the Christian centuries that followed, obsessed with the ideal of unity and with the difficulty of reconciling such a primal intuition with the multiplicity of contingent being. Plotinus posited the emanation from the immutable, undivided and transcendent One of two further principal 'hypostases': the Logos, which was the One reflecting upon itself and containing the divine Ideas or archetypes; and, thereunder, the World Soul, which sustained the visible world upon the model of those archetypes; the whole process of emanation remaining one continuum. The element of necessity in this emanational scheme, which can become a type of pantheism, did not commend it as a whole to Christian theologians of the early centuries or beyond: yet terminology indicative of emanation can be found even in Aquinas, and its inherent attraction lay in a seeming reconciliation of the transcendence of God with his immanence in creation. It is also easy to see how Plotinus's triad of hypostases would prove a tempting parallel to the Three-in-One processions of the Persons of the Trinity, despite the fact that the latter are equal and consubstantial, whereas neo-Platonic triads are hierarchically graded. Such triads are to be found in the Corpus Hermeticum as well. For centuries these writings were believed by many learned men to have been the inspired utterances of an Egyptian holy man, contemporary with Moses, who had inscribed his wisdom in mystical hieroglyphs; thus when Kircher came to interpret the hieroglyphs on the obelisks surviving in Rome it was an hermetic as well as a neo-Platonic message that he found in them, prelusive, as in the case of mystical triads, to the fuller revelation of Christianity. St Augustine too had given his blessing to the doctrine that there are vestiges of the Trinity in nature and man. In taking such views Kircher also showed himself the follower of Christian neo-Platonists of the Renaissance, such as Ficino and Pico della Mirandola.

It was figures like Ficino and Pico who were to draw out very fully the implications of a most important element in Platonism: its doctrine of participation. It is a doctrine that goes counter to any too easy a view of Platonism as dualistic and world-negating, and one briefly alluded to by Kircher in the last of the passages quoted. The allusion, significantly, is by way of a reference to Dionysius the Areopagite, the fifth century Christian neo-Platonist who, down till the 17th century, enjoyed vast *réclame* as a mystical theologian, since he was purported to have been that same Dionysius converted by St Paul in his speech on the Areopagus. Briefly, his cataphatic doctrine of participation held that the things of creation were greater or lesser images of the divine archetypes, or Ideas, in God. This notion is crystallised with admirable clarity by Philip Sherard in his sympathetic modern evocation of neo-Platonism. After insisting on the need to remember that such images of the divine are made by God out of his goodness, which they reflect in varied forms, so that the world is an image-world, a visible and changing expression of the invisible and the eternal, Sherard continues:

> *The Platonic universe is really a hierarchy of images, all co-existing, each issuing from and sharing in the one above it, from the highest supra-essential realities down to those of the visible world. It is this structure of participation which constitutes the great golden chain of being, that unbroken connection between the highest and lowest, heaven and earth. In this structure there is nothing that is not animate, nothing that is mere dead matter. All is endowed with being, all – even the least particle – belongs to a living transmuting whole.[7]*

The imagery of light so important in this tradition of Christian thought derives ultimately from the sun as image of the Good in Book VII of Plato's *Republic*, but this had become fused with a Biblical source so that the following passage from Dionysius the Areopagite communicates a vision of the universe as a comprehensively unified theophany:

> *Light comes from the Good, and light is an image of this archetypal Good . . . The great shining ever-lighting sun is the apparent image of the divine goodness, a distinct echo of the Good . . . The Good returns all things to itself and gathers together whatever may be scattered, for it is the divine source and unifier of the sum total of things . . . So it*

is with light, with the visible image of the Good. It draws and returns all things to itself, all the things that see, that have motion, that are receptive of illumination and warmth, that are held together by the spreading rays . . . Of course this ray never abandons its own proper nature or its interior unity. Even though it works itself outward to multiplicity and proceeds outside of itself as befits its generosity . . . nevertheless it remains inherently stable and is forever one with its own unchanging identity. And it grants to creatures the power to rise up, so far as they may, toward itself and it unifies them by way of its own simplified unity. Hence any thinking person realises that the appearances of beauty are signs of an invisible loveliness. The beautiful odours which strike the senses are representative of a conceptual diffusion. Material lights are images of the outpouring of an immaterial gift of light . . . the old myth used to describe the sun as the provident god and creator of this universe. I do not say this. But I do say that "ever since the creation of the world, the invisible things of God, his eternal power and deity, have been clearly perceived in the things that have been made".[8]

Despite the careful qualifications in that passage, it is clear that there lurks in it, as in all neo-Platonist participation and light-imagery, the possibility of an emanational pantheism. In the 9th Century A.D., three centuries after Dionysius, the mystical theologian John Scotus Erigena, who wrote at the court of Charles the Bald, Charlemagne's grandson, gave expression to the neo-Platonic Christian tradition, but in a manner that laid him open to just such a charge of pantheism, resulting in his condemnation by the Church. Yet despite his condemnation, a passage like the following, from his commentary on *The Celestial Hierarchy* of Dionysius the Areopagite, served to keep the tradition alive throughout the Middle Ages:

> *There is one God, one goodness, one light diffused throughout all things that are, so that they stand firm in their essences – a light shining in all things so that they may all be turned in loving meditation toward his beauty – excelling all things that are that all may delight in the plenitude of his perfection. In him all things are one. This stone, or this piece of wood to me is a light.*[9]

The divine nature, as Jon Whitman has observed, is for both Erigena and the Pseudo-Dionysius in one sense inaccessibly transcendent, but in another sense pervasively immanent.[10] That remark pinpoints a chronic paradox of the neo-Platonic Christian tradition down the ages. A dialectic of the two factors was constantly in play, and was to come to a climax in the 17th century Baroque period, which aspired to commingle straining polarities in a radiant union of earth with heaven: a *Coincidentia oppositorum* given theoretical utterance in the 15th century in the mystical metaphysics of Nicholas of Cusa, to whom we shall later turn.

In Scotus Erigena, along with the favourite light-imagery of Christian neo-Platonism, there are to be found texts concerning the pervasive harmony of the universe as a divine work of art constructed in terms of musical regularities, whereby the contrarieties and dissonances among different parts are reconciled;

and it is to such texts, with their sources in Antiquity and the early Christian Fathers, especially St Augustine, that we should relate Kircher's paragraph from *Musurgia Universalis* quoted at the beginning of this chapter. Similar harmonising factors of the tradition are developed by Otto von Simson in his book on the Gothic Cathedral. He traces them back to Dionysius the Areopagite and believes that they illuminate the iconographical programme of Abbot Suger for the first of the Gothic cathedrals in the 12th century. That century – during whose latter part such cathedrals emerged like vast chalices of light, the epitomes on earth of the heavenly Jerusalem constructed according to mathematical harmonies reflecting the *Musurgia Universalis* – also saw the flowering of the School of Chartres as a focus of neo-Platonism. Friedrich Heer has suggested that "a considerable part of the pantheism and nature cult of the renaissance and baroque was historically connected with the literary products of the cosmologists of Chartres".[11] Several other scholars have argued for the direct influence of the quasi-pantheist, Erigena, on one of the most famous products of the School of Chartres, the *Cosmographia* of Bernardus Sylvestris.

At one point, in a passage clearly influenced both by Plato's *Timaeus* and by Plotinus, Bernardus explores the notion that time is constantly being, as it were, gathered up into the eternal, into the vital unity of that total transcendence which is also total immanence.[12] Despite the linear and irreversible quality of time that Judaeo-Christianity set up in opposition to the cyclical doctrines of the ancient world, there is a sense in which Christianity did not abandon the cyclical. The framework formed by the creation and the end of the world can also be construed as a cycle. Time returns to eternity. In the 13th Century St Bonaventure, another Christian neo-Platonist, but one who post-dates the School of Chartres, can even make use of the symbol of the circle to argue that the Incarnation is a mystery of cosmic completion in which the circle of reality is brought to fulfilment by the conjunction of the first and the last. Between the lines of Christian eschatology there still breathed the spirit of circularity and cyclicity. Time remains 'non-linear'. Thus the ancient world's notion of cosmic harmony and unity was subsumed within Christian eschatolgy. And this surely chimes with what Auerbach had in mind when he wrote that in the Middle Ages contingent being in time is seen "not as a definite self-sufficient reality, not as a link in a chain of development in which single events or combinations of events perpetually give rise to new events, but viewed primarily in immediate vertical connection with a divine order".[13] Auerbach developed his theory in connection with Dante, another figure who has a place in any such discussion as this; as does Dante's mentor, St Thomas Aquinas.

Despite the efforts of many 20th century Thomists to 'existentialise' St Thomas, his affinities with the neo-Platonic tradition emerge not only in the occasional use of emanational terminology, but more extensively in his commentary on Dionysius the Areopagite's *De Divinis Nominibus*. In the words of Umberto Eco, the fourth chapter of *De Divinis Nominibus* "presents the universe as a cascade of beauties springing forth from the First Principle, a dazzling radiance of sensuous splendours in all created being".[14] The rhetorical emphasis of Eco's words invites a brief diversion, for it is a reminder that there is a sense in which this whole Christian neo-Platonic vision of existence is profoundly aesthetic. The epithet, however, must be taken in an extended sense; it is a vision wherein the cosmos is a great glittering icon, bodying forth the invisible beauty of its transcendent creator. Indeed the analogy between a work of art and the cosmos was of frequent occurrence throughout the whole period from late antiquity to the 17th century, and derived from St Augustine, for whom suffering and evil were the dissonances necessary for the harmony of the whole. Sheer base matter had dubious ontological status, if any. The Saint expressed himself thus: "God, who is the unchangeable Governor as he is the unchangeable Creator of mutable things, orders all events in his Providence until the beauty of the completed course of time, of which the component parts are the dispensations adapted to each successive age, shall be finished like the grand melody of some ineffably wise master of song".[15] St Thomas, from whom we briefly turned aside, used the text of the Areopagite to sum up his own sense of the unity and harmony which pervade the cosmic artefact of the Divine Wisdom. The latter, as he puts it, "transmits to all creatures, with a certain lightning-like brightness, a ray of His own brilliant light, which is the source of all illumination."[16] Those words of St Thomas recall many a passage in Dante's *Paradiso*, where the whole universe is pervaded in varying degrees by the supernal light which is its native medium. One of Dante's modern commentators, George Holmes, makes the point that under the influence of neo-Platonic thought, the tendency of this picture of the universe was to blunt the characteristic distinction between God on the one hand and creation on the other, so that the universe is a "harmonious system of spiritual influences":[17]

That which not dieth and that which can die
Reflect but that idea in their gleam
Which in His love our Sire begets on high.
That living radiance which so sends its beam
From its bright source, that it parts not from it
Nor from the Love that is en-threed with them,
Doth of its bounty its own rays unite,
As though in a mirror, in nine subsistences,
Itself remaining one eternal light.
Thence it descends to the least potencies
Downward from act to act, becoming soon
Such as makes only brief contingencies.
And these contingencies may well be shown
To be the things engendered by the stress
Of moving heaven, from seed or else unsown.
Their wax and that which doth the wax impress
Vary; beneath the ideal stamp we find,
Therefore, a brilliance now more and now less . . . [18]

In that passage the pre-Copernican cosmology seems the perfect physical correlate of God's spiritual relation to His creation. In a later Canto, however, (*Paradiso* XXVIII, 13-78), a paradoxical inversion occurs. Dante, having reached the *Primum Mobile*, at the outer rim of the circular Ptolemaic cosmos, fastens his eyes on a point beyond; and around that point, which is God, the angelic hierarchies are ranged in widening circles. The one circular effect seems to contradict the other. Where is the centre to be found?

Singleton, in his commentary on the *Paradiso*, thinks that "the whole matter can be most simply stated in terms of circumference and centre. Up to now we have been moving with the wayfarer within a universe that has the motionless earth as the centre, and 'the mind of God', the Empyrean, as the circumference. But now, in this symbolic vision, the centre is shown to be a point, which is God, the circumference is the order of angels which preside over the sphere of the moon – and the earth is nowhere!"[19] Singleton's gloss makes us aware of the paradox latent in the image of circularity that the Christian world had inherited from the cosmology of antiquity. The elements of paradox are hinted at as far back as Plotinus where he remarked that "all beings may be thought of as centres uniting at one central centre . . . "; and, a little later, stressing the notion of unity, "a true unity must in some way be able to manifest itself as including the contrary nature, that of potential multiplicity, while by the fact that this multiplicity belongs to it not as from without but as from and by itself, it remains authentically one, possessing boundlessness and multiplicity within that nature; its nature must be such that it can appear as a whole at every point."[20] The full implication for Christian mystical theology of the paradox which Plotinus hints at appears in the 12th century in a brief but famous and influential formula from a pseudo-Hermetic work entitled *Liber XXIV Philosophorum*: "God is an infinite sphere whose centre is everywhere and circumference nowhere". This metaphor, which was eventually to lead European thought beyond the medieval cosmos, and was to be a stimulus to Giordano Bruno's post-Copernican vision of the infinitude of the physical universe, became a commonplace by the 16th and 17th centuries, even among those who – like Athanasius Kircher – did not accept the Copernican and Galilean cosmology.

There was one later medieval thinker, whom Kircher certainly assimilated, who explored to the utmost the implications of the famous hermetic formula. This was the Christian 15th century neo-Platonist metaphysician and theologian, Nicholas of Cusa. In a striking way Nicholas followed through the implications of the relation between immanence and transcendence so central to neo-Platonism by transferring the hermetic paradox from God to the world. Perhaps it would be more accurate to say that he pursued the inter-penetration of the world and God to a bold extreme, but without lapsing into heresy. Wherever a man might be, Nicholas averred, he might believe himself to be at the centre of the world: "In movement there is no absolute minimum, like a fixed centre, since necessarily the minimum and the maximum are identical. Now the world has no circumference . . . Since, then, the world cannot be enclosed within a material circumference and centre, it is unintelligible without God as its centre and circumference. It is not infinite, yet it cannot be conceived as finite, since there are no limits within which it is enclosed."[21]

In phrasing which echoes John Scotus Erigena, Nicholas holds that the world is a theophany, a 'contraction' of the divine being.[22] The universe is the *Contractum Maximum* which came into being through emanation from the *Absolutum Maximum* who is God. He holds that God is the essence of the world and that the universe is that essence in a state of contraction: "Since the universe restricted is in each actually existing individual, then evidently God, who is in the universe, is in every individual and every individual actually existing is, like the universe, immediately in God".[23] Nicholas abandoned the traditional Aristotelian and Thomistic hierarchical universe, and the tenor of his writing suggests an immense dynamic whole in which everything depends on everything, reworking the ancient pre-Socratic intuition of Anaxagoras: *quodlibet esse in quolibet.* Kircher, in his pilgrimage amid the constellations, *Itinerarium Ecstaticum*, makes exactly that point: ". . . For though the world is inconceivable and immeasurable in extent, and the stars innumerable, yet all things are in all things, and each single thing is through some ineffable reason in every other single thing, *quodlibet in quolibet*".[24] It is interesting to note that in other closely related passages of the same work Kircher, who knows he has Nicholas of Cusa as a precedent, seems anxious to distance himself from the Cardinal, whose views on the *Absolutum Maximum* (God) and the *Absolutum Contractum* (the world) he mistrusts, presumably because of their pantheistic possibilities.

It will be clear by now how closely Nicholas of Cusa might appear to have sailed to a type of pantheism. It was this lesson which Giordano Bruno was to derive from his writings a century later. Nothing, however, could have been further from the intention of the pious Cardinal of Cusa. He was simply exploring to the limit the paradoxes of participation inherent in the neo-Platonic tradition, within a context that was moreover deeply incarnational and Christological. For Nicholas the only truly adequate nexus between the divine Infinite and the cosmic Indefinite – for so he is careful to distinguish them – lay in the divine humanity of Christ. Kircher follows Nicholas of Cusa on this subject too, and does so in precisely the same terminology. Thus in the *Itinerarium Ecstaticum* he explains that Christ is both the *Maximum Absolutum* as well as that *Maximum* in a state of contraction.[25] The debts of a writer like Kircher to Nicholas of

Cusa are readily understandable, for despite the paradoxes of the Cusan's metaphysics and theology and despite his forward-looking epistemology and Renaissance attitude to the creative power of human knowledge, Nicholas retained, and could indeed be said to consummate the vision of Christian neo-Platonic harmony and unity. "It seems," wrote Maurice de Gandillac, "that within the Cusan all the great intuitions of Platonism took on all their religious and metaphysical value."[26]

"The great intuitions of Platonism": transcendence and immanence; creation and participation; reflection of the One in the Many, and of the eternal in the temporal; the impulse to synthesise and unify; the unifying and all-pervasive metaphor of light. These themes were further enriched by the neo-Platonism of the Florentine Academy in the late 15th century, and the writings of men such as Marsilio Ficino and Pico della Mirandola fed the ever-widening stream that was to debouch into the writings of Athanasius Kircher in the mid-17th century.

Ficino and Pico, as well as taking up traditional Platonic themes of universal harmony animated by love, governed by circular emanation and return to a transcendent centre, and sealed by Christian revelation, were avid synthesisers of the "Prisci Theologi". This group, which includes both historical and mythical figures who were seen as precursors of the perennial truths of religion to be crowned by Christian revelation, was an ever-proliferating source of learned analogies and cross-referencing – Orphic, Pythagorean, Chaldaic, Egyptian – on the part of Renaissance and Baroque polymaths. Eminent among the *Prisci Theologi* was the mythical Hermes Trismegistus, whose purported writings, the *Corpus Hermeticum*, had been translated from Greek into Latin by Ficino. Mention has already been made of Hermes Trismegistus as a favourite source of quotation for Athanasius Kircher. Kircher was obviously familiar not only with the Greek original but with Ficino's exegesis, and a passage from his *Oedipus Aegyptiacus* echoes Ficino and reveals the Christian syncretist in the Baroque polymath:

> *Hermes Trismegistus, as first originator of hieroglyphs . . .*
> *was the first and most venerable of all among the Egyptians*
> *who reasoned rightly in divine matters. From him originated*
> *whatever was worthily set forth concerning God by*
> *Orpheus, Musaeus, Homerus, Euripides and others, as the*
> *orthodox memorials of the Holy Fathers more than*
> *sufficiently show as well.*[27]

In the same work, after a long quotation on God from the *Pimander*, a section of the *Corpus Hermeticum*, Kircher exclaims, "Who, I ask, can find for us a Christian who speaks more loftily and more correctly about God? Which theologian has a profounder perception of divine things? Certainly all these things are to be found expressed most aptly in hieroglyphics . . ."[28] In hieroglyphics, Kircher proceeds, Hermes Trismegistus had directly inscribed the mysteries of divinity unmediated by the necessity of discursive thought; a point of view which had first been given classic formulation by Plotinus in the Third Century A.D.

The attraction to hidden mysteries, which nevertheless always lead back to the substantial unity of faith, evident in the fascination with hieroglyphs, also accounts for the attraction to the Jewish Cabbala.

Plate 4: Athanasius Kircher, Oedipus Aegyptiacus, *Frontispiece (Romae, 1652–5)*

Kircher, clad in garb suggestive of Roman triumph, extends his right hand in a gesture of eloquent revelation towards a demure-looking sphinx surmounting a rocky plinth; an oriental palm-tree curvaceously abuts. The efficacy of Kircher's Egyptological studies is shown as having its origin in the two figures that hover above his head: Experience and Reason. The latter clasps a scroll indicating the polyglot sources of Kircher's wisdom.

This was prominent in Ficino's follower, Pico della Mirandola, as well as in Giles of Viterbo, head of the Augustinian order in early 16th century Rome. The latter's writings possibly inspired the iconography of the Sistine vault and certainly played a crucial role in the apotheosizing of papal Rome. Governing the belief of men like Ficino, Pico, Giles, and of course Kircher, was the faith in a system of primitive theology everywhere harmonious with itself, such consistency being a token of truth. These theological-cum-metaphysical-cum-hermetical syntheses were a last colossal flourish of the ingrained tendency of Christian neo-Platonism, now studded with the magical and animistic accretions especially prominent since the Renaissance, to see the universe as an intricately interwoven system of signs and correspondences, a terrain upon which the imprint of the living god, the *Vestigia Dei*, was everywhere apparent:

Therefore in the being of all things we can wonder at the power of God the Creator; in their truth venerate the wisdom of the artificer; in their goodness love the generosity of the lover, in their unity comprehend as it were the unique simplicity of the Creator, who has united each single thing within himself, and all things among themselves . . .

Everything that is in the totality of worlds also exists in each single one, nor is there any one of them which does not participate in all of the rest; and if we wish to be assured of the truth of this, it was, I think, the opinion of Anaxagoras, as expounded by the Pythagoreans and the Platonists.[29]

Those quotations from Pico della Mirandola, the former from his *De Ente et Uno*, the latter from *Heptaplus*, his commentary on the days of creation, clearly exemplify the ideal of cosmic harmony and unity which was a *leit-motif* of Christian neo-Platonism. The *Heptaplus* reminds us that the Renaissance and Baroque periods were also periods in which the hexaemeral theme was especially prominent in the arts. The six biblical days of creation were the inspiration of innumerable variations on the splendours of the physical world seen as Vestigia Dei, and the following passage from Weingartner's *Der Geist des Barock* well captures the celestial exuberance that pervades so many works of art of the High Renaissance and Baroque periods:

> *The baroque period took for granted a belief in a future perfection and transfiguration of life, and this faith, instinct with hope, so far from damping in any way its enjoyment of the natural life, precisely gave to that life its value and price. Hence the joyousness, the splendour, the flood of light in which baroque art clothes even this earthly existence; hence the cheerful affirmation of all reality, including that of matter; hence the ease with which every natural means of expression was pressed into the service of religious art; hence the disappearance of all strict boundaries between the world above and that below, since everyone was convinced that there was no gap between spirit and matter, between nature and supernatural, between heaven and earth; that, on the contrary, the one builds on the other, that, in fact, they complete each other.*[30]

Baroque culture indeed gave tremendous amplitude to depictions of the physical world, but the Baroque amplitude is always dramatically suffused with light, traditional symbol of the celestial origins of the physical universe. It was the imaginative culmination of that theme of the immanence of the divine and eternal in the things of time which was so prominent in Christian neo-Platonism down the centuries. Indeed Hans Urs von Balthasar could write even of the theology of the Jesuits that "the relation of reciprocity between God and the world (has) a cosmic amplitude which, in the final contemplation of the Exercises, strikes a very 'Areopagitican' note".[31]

The glory of God in creation, so prominent in High Renaissance art under the revived inspiration of the neo-Platonising Greek Fathers of the early Church, especially of a work like St Basil's *Hexaemeron*, can thus be seen as a theme which persisted through and beyond the Counter-Reformation. The Counter-Reformation naturally had its elements of austerity and repression, but these were by no means its only important aspect; Catholic Baroque culture of the period is as well represented by Cardinal Bellarmine's *The Mind's Ascent to God*, an eloquent panegyric of the visible splendours of divine creativity, as by his *Art of Dying Well*, a more traditionally medieval theme. The wonderful sentences at the end of Burckhardt's *Civilization of the Renaissance in Italy* encapsulate something of the open and affirmative sensibility that spans both High Renaissance and Baroque. It leads Burckhardt to conclude that "the visible world was created by God in love, that it is the copy of a pattern pre-existing in Him, and that He will ever remain its eternal mover and restorer. The soul of man can by recognising God draw Him into narrow boundaries, but also by love to Him itself expand into the Infinite – and this is blessedness on earth".[32]

The deepest intuition in Christian neo-Platonic immanence and cosmic harmony is that of the universe as an all-encompassing theophany. It is a vision of Paradise. Tasso's *Il Mondo Creato* was in its day one of the most famous of late Renaissance hexaemeral poems. In Book 7 of the work Tasso – who prefigured so much of Baroque opulence as well as Baroque fugacity – speculates on the four rivers of Paradise, whence they sprang and whither they flow. The Book concludes with a vision of many of the elements of that paradisal setting, which included features such as these: "Gracious rivers and fountains were heard to murmur His sacred, glorious name. Birds of the air and darting fishes, and beasts both tame and wild, blended their praises in songful radiance. Priests, in majestic temples, uttered His praise in deep-toned song".

This was not, be it noted, merely a rural and bucolic Eden but a place of temples and fountains too; and it was just some such paradisal image that, from the 15th century until the Baroque period, governed papal plans for the rebuilding of Rome, the holy city, as a visible image of the divine and the eternal. Emblems that epitomise union with the divine lie all around Rome, and one such instance is the Fountain of the Four Rivers in Piazza Navona. Biblical as well as Christian neo-Platonic symbolism is to be found there, and the monument's guiding spirit, at least in so far as the crowning obelisk and its hieroglyphs are concerned, was Athanasius Kircher. One product of Kircher's association with this fountain was *Obeliscus Pamphilius*, which he wrote at the suggestion of the Pamphili pope, Innocent X.

Plate 5 Piazza Navona, Rome: Bernini's Four Rivers Fountain, with
Obelisk

This work, as well as illustrating in detail Kircher's erroneous interpretation of the hieroglyphs along Christian neo-Platonic and hermetic lines, offered a vast preliminary summation of all current learning of that type – though nothing like as vast as the monstrously comprehensive *Oedipus Aegyptiacus*, which followed a few years later. The commission for the actual design and execution of the fountain went to Bernini, an artist recently returned to papal favour solely by virtue of the triumphant submission of such a design. It is tempting to speculate that Kircher's influence extended to more than the interpretation of the hieroglyphs on the obelisk. He was, after all, Rome's most eminent scholar and one of the most famous learned men of the age, and it would not be wonderful if the symbolism which informs other aspects of this work owed something to the interaction between the Baroque artist and the Jesuit syncretist. And to a limited extent, as Kaspar Schott's preamble to *Obeliscus Pamphilius* makes clear, such interaction did in fact take place.

That a holy mountain stands at the centre of the world, representing the union of heaven and earth, is an ancient mythological belief, and the grotto-enclosing tumulus whence the waters flow in Bernini's *concetto* of the Four Rivers incorporates this archetype. Closer to a specifically Christian theme are the iconographical possibilities of the four rivers which rose, as everyone knew, from the mountain of Paradise. Paradise was the symbol of the original justified state of mankind, and in one of the inscriptions for the monument that Kircher anthologised in a historical overview prefacing *Obeliscus Pamphilius*, paradisal associations are linked with the spiritual renewal to be anticipated from the pontificate of Innocent X:

> *Innocent X in the holy year of justice restored, poured forth*
> *four rivers of the ancient paradise from one fountain of*
> *virgin water, that is to say, he gives visible proof of justice,*
> *and renews the age.*

Finally, Petrucci's contemporary panegyrical poem, *Pamphilia Gens*, shows how clear the basic *concetto* of the fountain was to contemporary eyes:

> *Look upon the Forum Agonalis and you will behold a*
> *wonder of the world – what vast rivers the world has in her*
> *bosom. From the fountain of rocks burst forth the four huge*
> *rivers of the globe, which Paradise puts forth. Here the*
> *Nile, and here gem-bearing Ganges pay worship to Rome,*
> *Tigris and Euphrates flow beneath our yoke.*[33]

The foliage around the base of the fountain is surely paradisal in its suggestion of exuberant fertility and regeneration. To this one should link the obelisk itself: traditionally a fertilising sun-symbol in Egyptian religion. In papal Rome, however, and under the guiding inspiration of the syncretising Kircher, it was much more than a sun-symbol. Kircher refers in *Obeliscus Pamphilius* to the hieroglyphs of the *Numen Triform* at the top of the obelisk, the prime mystery of the Egyptian cult, as prefigurations of the Christian Trinity, and envisages it, by some blurring of the Holy Spirit with an *anima mundi* concept, as "descending into multiplicity from its solitary unity it engenders life, movement, force in every lower being, diffusing itself in the four regions of the universe, indicated by the four sides of the obelisk".[34] It would not be amiss here to remember as well the mystagogical associations of the number '4' in Pythagoreanism, where the primal monad acts upon latent matter comprising four elements, the whole cosmos being conceived as a derivative of the number '4'.

Such arcane considerations, certainly to be anticipated among the learned cognoscenti of the age, would have gained contemporary resonance by virtue of the expanding missionary activities of the post-Tridentine Church. With the aid of the recently founded congregation Propaganda Fide, the Church aspired to bring all four continuents within the orbit of Rome, *mundus umbilicus* and cosmic centre. The papal arms, held aloft by one of the allegorical figures that represent the four rivers, and thus the four continents they water, assert, heraldically, this universal sovereignty.

The attitudes of the four 'continent' figures, concentric to the central vertical of the obelisk, with its culminating emblem of the dove, are significantly varied. The Danube, – Europe as prime bearer of Christian culture, with its accompanying emblem of the horse – is wholly turned towards the source of divine salvation, and supports the papal arms; the River Plate, symbol of an American continent only half-emerged from heathen darkness, makes a gesture of avoidance, yet also of dazzlement at the divine source of truth; the Nile of Africa partially veils its face and yet is also supportive of the papal arms; Ganges – Asia – is turned self-sufficiently away from the rest, since missionary activities in that part of the world were seriously impeded.

The interpretation given above, by Pochat,[35] is neither conclusive nor exhaustive but does cover some of the more plausible contemporary dimensions of the whole *concetto*. There are, and always were, other emphases. Rudolf Preimesberger[36] sees the exhilarating upward-sweeping curve of Africa's gigantic palm-tree, which is such a crucially integrating feature of the visual ensemble, as a theological symbol forming, together with the snake on the edge of the fountain and the dove at the apex of the obelisk, an iconographical cluster that pays tribute to the Pamphili pope in a way that adds weight to what is already a clamorously papal monument.

Plate 6: Bernini: Fountain of the Four Rivers (detail)

It is not, surely, merely papal, in the sense of being just a monument to a heraldically inclined potentate. There has been scholarly dispute about this: one writer[37] seeing the monument as primarily a Pamphili affair; others, whom I follow, taking it as far more comprehensively theological. That obelisk with its crowning papal family emblem is admittedly a representation of the Pamphili dove holding an olive branch in its beak, but is also, and far more importantly, an emblem of the Holy Spirit. Take Athanasius Kircher for our guide and we shall see that the Four Rivers Fountain with its obelisk is not just a monument to papal family pride, nor even to expanding Catholicism, but epitomises a whole tradition of syncretising neo-Platonic Catholicism: it gives visual expression to the predilection for unity, harmony and light in that tradition of Christian thought and sensibility.

Obelisks embodied, for the learned theological eclectics of the Renaissance and Baroque, a primordial spiritual symbolism. An obelisk was a sun-symbol and, taken from base to apex, implied a transition from the earthly human world to incorporeal divinity itself. This origin in a solar cult, where it represented the diffusion of light, made it a useful symbol for the neo-Platonic Christian tradition to exploit and elaborate. The widening of the four sides from a narrower apex symbolised the rays of the sun. That triangular apex in turn, when combined with the diffusion of light, was apt to symbolise the Holy Trinity of the Christian revelation, so that, as Kircher puts it in *Obeliscus Pamphilius:*

> *All things conspire to signify the Trinity; for, as has been*
> *shown elsewhere, the triangle is the symbol of the Sacred*
> *Triad: it is placed on the apex, that is, the highest point of*

the obelisk, just like the tripliform high God, whose emanational influence opens out as if from the incomprehensible centre of all things into the breadth of the material world as toward a circumference (as is beautifully shown by the rays of the four sides spread outward from the topmost point of the obelisk toward the base, as it were towards a broad kingdom) . . . From these influences the richness and abundance of all things necessary for human life emanate. And this too is that linking of these worlds which Plato and Pythagoras mention as being established by the Egyptians. Since indeed the obelisk with its four sides corresponds with the four parts of the globe.[38]

Kircher there comes close to equating the *vis penetrativa* of the Egyptian solar cult with the action of the Holy Spirit, which in turn comes close to associating the Holy Spirit with the *Anima Mundi* of the neo-Platonists; this last a not unknown aberration of some of the early Fathers. Kircher's mind was not a sharp analytical instrument, but rather a receptively associative one. He uses the notion of emanation, whose origins in Plotinus were touched on above, as if unaware of its pantheistic and necessitarian dangers. He does so for the good reason that it never occurred to him that the inspiring and suggestive terminology of any of the *Prisci Theologi* – the Hermeticists, the neo-Platonists, the Cabbalists, the Pythagoreans – was not providentially intended to be incorporated within the light of Christian revelation, the decisiveness of which he, as a Jesuit, never doubted. One of the most comprehensively syncretising passages in his writings – and he was primarily an encyclopedist and rhetorician – gathers up much of the neo-

Platonising Christian theology he had imbibed, along with its imagery of the emanation of divine light. The passage is to be found not in *Obeliscus Pamphilius* but in *Ars Magna Lucis et Umbrae*, and over its ending there hovers a sense of the universe as one great celestial organism animated by divine light and heat. It is thus a reminder of how much Christian neo-Platonism owed to Stoicism and the hermetic doctrines, and an object lesson in how the transcendent creator-God of Judaeo-Christian revelation was infiltrated by the timeless ideals of unity, harmony and light which were central to the cosmic religion of the ancient world:

> *According to the ancient theologians the Supreme Spirit is an infinite light from which (being immaterial) that first immaterial light shines forth which is the reflection of the paternal depths: this light is then sent forth to all true substances. All these things Christian theologians apply to the sacramental action of the most holy Trinity: so that thus the infinite light is the eternal Father; the light from light is the Son, or ray as it were of the divine substance and the reflection of the paternal glory; from which the Holy Spirit proceeds as heat warming the realm of essences and thence the whole world by the fire of its heat.*[39]

In all Christian neo-Platonism there is a fundamental leaning towards the timeless, since the imagery of emanation and return tends to mitigate the contingencies of historical mutability and to enfold all things within the circle of a perfectly unified and harmonious cosmos, the expression of the divine in all its parts. If we were to seek a formal philosophical system which in the 17th century period of the Baroque consummated such a primal ontological intuition of cosmic harmony, it might seem best found in the philosophy of Leibniz, whose thought bears an interesting resemblance, in certain respects, to that of Nicholas of Cusa: a plurality of monads, each a centre to itself but contributing to the comprehensive harmony of the whole and dependent upon God, the supreme Monad – "born every moment by continual fulgurations from the divinity", as Leibniz puts it, in words reminiscent of the pseudo-Dionysius.[40] Hans Barth, writing from within the tradition of German *Geistesgeschichte*, has seen in Leibniz the pre-eminent philosopher of the Baroque, in whose *Monadology* the ancient ideal of harmonious wholeness achieved its apotheosis.[41] There is, however, too much in Leibniz' thought that gives a foretaste of the 18th century Enlightenment, as well as of Romanticism, to make it a satisfactory symbol of traditional Christian ontology as reflected in the peculiar conditions of the Baroque phase of European culture. Moreover, the artistic products of a cultural era go beyond the parameters of any retrospective conceptual scheme, and their claims upon us retain an irreducible individuality. Such, I think, must ultimately be the response to anyone trying to link – as I have done – a cultural monument like Bernini's Fountain of the Four Rivers and its obelisk to a tradition of thought that culminates in Bernini's exact contemporary, and interpreter of the obelisk, Athanasius Kircher.

For a more visually nuanced approach let us turn to the French literary critic, Jean Rousset. Rousset has beautifully caught the individual complexity of the Fountain of the Four Rivers. He has grasped something which goes beyond timeless stability and harmony and yet is just as endemic to the Baroque 'moment' in

European culture: something mobile and fugacious whose nature, along with other more decisive elements of tension, I shall touch on in my fourth chapter. The words qualify any too facile an identification of Baroque culture with the stabilising traditional rhetoric of a Kircher. Rousset writes:

> *Around and beneath a motionless centre – the vertical of the obelisk which, in the allegorical language of the age, symbolises eternity – there is spread out the moving circle of natural rocks and flowing water with its reflections, around which revolve the emblems of the rivers and the animals, where plants are bent by the wind, and where the stone supports are hewn and perforated cross-wise (– as the preparatory drawings show even more clearly). Thus, in this nexus of contrasting relationships, the lower diagonals are subordinated to the highest vertical, the cavity to the needle which it supports, flowingness to solidity, and – subordinated to the stable, the instability of the enormous slashed, slanting water-borne base . . .* [It is] crucial to sense everywhere the simultaneous presence of two poles of attraction *and, at the same time, the linking action – from the One to the many and from the many to the One, from the unstable to the stable and* vice versa *– of a visible circulation which ensures that between the divergent or disparate elements of the whole there exists the homogeneity, the continuity of one current.*[42]

The 'current' to which Rousset refers is something that the sympathetic viewer must surely experience as his eye is swept upwards by the giant palm-tree – a symbol of victory, beloved of

Baroque artists for its curving strength and the flourish of its fronds – and directed from the base of the obelisk to the crowning Pamphili dove, the emblem of a reigning Pope. Such a Pope is more than the representative of a ruling family, though he was certainly that at this period; he was and is also the very same being to whom Our Lord said *Tu es Petrus*. These words, inscribed in colossal gold mosaic lettering inside the vault of St Peter's, are an awesome reminder that it is the Pope who, under the Holy Spirit, timelessly mediates to the Church, and thence to the city and the world, the message of universal salvation. The Catholic mentality of that period would find no difficulty in accepting the dove both as a piece of papal heraldry emblematic of princely benevolence, and as a theological image symbolic of the Holy Spirit. This would especially be the case in a culture where the papacy was still acutely aware of its quasi-dynastic rôle as inheritor of the providentially guided *Imperium* of Rome and its universalist claims. Fagiolo dell'Arco, in his account of the Four Rivers Fountain as a triumphalist monument, hints at the nexus of papal and imperial Rome which will be the theme of the following chapter:

> *The pope triumphs over the changing appearances of life. But he triumphs also over the Elements: water (represented by a symbol like the Four Rivers, but also living water, splashing or calm), air (see the wind which tangles in the branches of the palm), earth (the changing rocks which contain the varied human figures . . .) And it will not be too bold to see also the triumph of the Pope over the characters of mankind symbolised at that period (see for instance the*

Iconologia of Ripa) precisely by the four elements. The Nile, for example, is sacred on account of its beneficent flooding, the Ganges receives the rites of India and is also the incarnation of the god Vishna, the River Plate is a means of communication and a fountain of life for wide areas . . . At the centre of Piazza Navona a monument is born which celebrates papal triumph over difficulty, life and the elements: which reconciles the sacred with the pagan just as the 'innocent dove' (of which the inscription speaks) reconciles the Holy Spirit and the papal arms.[43]

In that passage – admittedly bordering on the fanciful – we nevertheless catch a rewarding glimpse not just of the papal but also of what one might call the archetypal meaning of the Four Rivers Fountain and its obelisk: a symbol of the dream, recurrent in the history of humanity, of a harmonious cosmos having at its centre a holy city that conciliates all elements, joins earth to heaven, cancels the ravages of time, and re-integrates all things within the timeless circle of the sacred.

Notes to Chapter II

1. M. de Gandillac, 'Pascal et le Silence du Monde', in *Blaise Pascal: L'Homme et l'Oeuvre* (Les Editions de Minuit, 1956) 346

2. F.W. Dilliston, *Christianity and Symbolism* (London, 1955) 80

3. A. Kircher, *Arithmologia* (Romae, 1665) 262-3

4. A. Kircher, *Musurgia Universalis* (Romae, 1650) 390-1. [Translated in J. Godwin, *Music, Mysticism and Magic*, Arkana, 1986.]

5. A. Kircher, *Ars Magna Lucis et Umbrae* (Romae, 1646) 796

6. A. Kircher, *Obeliscus Pamphilius* (Romae, 1650) 211

7. Philip Sherard, *The Eclipse of Man and Nature* (Lindisfarne Press, 1987) 24

8. Pseudo-Dionysius, *The Complete Works* ed. P. Rorem, tr. C. Luibheid (Paulist Press, 1987) 74-5 . . . 146

9. *Patrologia Latina*, CXXII ed. J.-P. Migne, columns 128-9

10. J. Whitman, *Allegory* (Oxford, 1987) 159

11. F. Heer, *The Intellectual History of Europe* (Weidenfeld and Nicolson, 1966) 110

12. cf. B. Stock, *Myth and Science in the 12th Century* (Princeton, 1972) 142-3

13. E. Auerbach, *'Figura', Scenes from the Drama of European Literature* (Meridian Books 1959) 72

14. Umberto Eco, *The Aesthetics of St Thomas Aquinas* (Radius, USA, 1988) 23

15. St Augustine, *Epistle CLXXXVIII*

16. St Thomas Aquinas, *De Divinis Nominibus* (IV 5)

17. G. Holmes, *Dante* (OUP 1980) 39

18. *Dante's Paradiso* tr. L. Binyon (London 1952) 149-150

19. *The Divine Comedy*, tr. and ed. C.S. Singleton (Princeton, 1975) 450

20. *The Enneads* VI (5), tr. S. MacKenna (Faber, 1969) 535-538

21. *On Learned Ignorance* II (XI) tr. E. Heron (Routledge and Kegan Paul, 1954) 107

22. cf. F. Copleston, *History of Philosophy* Volume III (London, 1964) 239

23. *On Learned Ignorance* II (5)

24. *Iter Ecstaticum Coeleste* (Nuremberg, 1660) 397. (A later edition of *Itinerarium Ecstaticum.*)

25. *Iter*, 453-4

26. Gandillac, op. cit., 359

27. *Oedipus Aegyptiacus* (Romae, 1652-4) 568

28. ibid., 505

29. *Pico della Mirandola*, ed. E. Garin (Valecchi Editore, 1942) 432-689

30. Quoted in L. Pastor, *History of the Popes* Vol. XXVII tr. E. Graf (London, 1938) 13-14

31. Hans Urs von Balthasar, *La Gloire et La Croix: Le Domaine de la Métaphysique: Les Constructions* (Aubier, 1982) 164

32. J. Burckhardt, *The Civilisation of the Renaissance in Italy* (Phaidon Press) 292

33. cf. R. Preimesberger, 'Obeliscus Pamphilius', *Münchner Jahrbuch für Kunstgeschichte*, 3rd Series, Vol. XXV, 1974

34. *Obeliscus Pamphilius* (Romae, 1650) 395

35. G. Pochat, 'Uber Berninis "Concetto" zum Vierströmbrunnen auf Piazza Navona', *Konsthistorik Tidskrift* (35) 1966

36. Preimesberger, op. cit., 140-1

37. N. Huse, 'La Fontaine des Fleuves du Bernini', *Revue de l'Art* (7) 1970, 6-17

38. *Obeliscus Pamphilius*, 409 . . . 396

39. *Ars Magna Lucis et Umbrae*, 796

40. G.W. Leibniz, *The Monadology*, para. 47

41. Hans Barth. 'Das Zeitalter des Barocks und die Philosophie von Leibniz', *Die Kunstformen des Barockzeitalters* (Bern, 1956)

42. 'Saint-Yves et les Poètes', in *L'Intérieur et L'Extérieur*, (Paris, 1976) 260-1 (my emphasis). cf. also, Roger Scruton: "It is only a superficial reading of architectural Baroque (namely Portoghesi's) which identifies the destabilising and fragmenting elements as the most important. The Baroque arose from a religious idea. It was an attempt to spiritualise the forms of architecture, by incorporating into them heavenly representation of themselves: infected by change and process, but also immutable. It depended on, and endorsed, the classical forms and details – column, pilaster, architraves, mouldings – which are the tokens of immortality, set amid the things of this world, always moving, yet eternally still". (Times Literary Supplement 18.12.92).

43. M. e M. Fagiolo dell'Arco, *Bernini, une Introduzione al gran teatro del barocco* (Roma, 1967) 90.

CHAPTER III

ROMA AETERNA

The heraldic device of Pope Innocent X, which crowns the obelisk of the Fountain of the Four Rivers, consists of a dove holding an olive branch in its beak, and three lilies. Dove, olive-branch and lilies were also the emblems of Venus, Athene, and Juno respectively; thus united, they would have directed the minds of heraldic and mythological cognoscenti to the ultimate harmony that emerged between Juno and Venus as a result of their active rôles in the destiny of Aeneas, the hero of Vergil's epic on the founding of the Roman Empire.[1]

In that very same Piazza Navona of the Four Rivers Fountain there is another more extended reminder of the analogy which was current in the 17th century between the Papacy and the Roman Empire. At the southern end of the square is the family palace of the Pamphili pope, where the main gallery is decorated by Pietro da Cortona with scenes from Vergil's *Aeneid*. Carefully chosen to show the trials and ultimate triumph of Aeneas and his companions, these scenes foreshadow the blessedness of the

Augustan world-order, and portend the providentially guided destiny of the Church. That same Roman Empire was designed by Providence to unite a diversity of peoples in the known world as a universal setting for the birth of the Saviour who, in founding the Church, entrusted its guidance to one supreme pastor, St Peter. St Peter in turn was to found the ecclesiological imperium of the papacy, which continued and completed, on a vastly extended scale, the task of bringing all humankind into one fold: its centre Rome, the new Jerusalem of the modern age. Thus the Pamphili emblem, on the top of the Four Rivers obelisk, as well as symbolising the Holy Spirit, is also suggestive, particularly when linked with the *Aeneid* frescoes in the nearby Pamphili Palace, of the imperial mission of the Papacy. The traditional links between Empire and Papacy which the post-Tridentine Church inherited were such, that what might well appear today to be family self-glorification on the part of the Pamphili pope was actually something more subtle. It was part of a whole set of ecclesiological beliefs, with roots which went back to the early centuries of the faith, persisted throughout the Middle Ages and proliferated wonderfully during the High Renaissance and the Baroque. The providential destiny of the Church linked all things Roman: imperial, catholic and papal.

The pope who preceded Innocent X, Bernini's Urban VIII, made this whole cluster of beliefs evident in a poem written when he was still Cardinal Maffeo Barberini, on the occasion of the completion under Paul V (Borghese) of the façade of the new St Peter's. The title of the poem is *Religionis orthodoxae primordia per Apostolorum Principes Petrum et Paulum constituta*. Here the Cardinal, prompted by the completion of the façade of the basilica, reflects on the marvellous expansion of the Empire as the seat of a world-wide Catholic faith. Next, turning to the story of Aeneas, he sees Jupiter's abandonment of Priam and the Trojans, and his election of Aeneas, as a rehearsal for the triumph of the Church over the Synagogue. Such, then, was the climate of ideas; and it is still not amiss, when one stands at the main entrance of St Peter's and gazes down the great nave at Bernini's Baldachin and the view beyond, where it so imperiously frames the *Cathedra Petri*, to sense an element of Roman triumph in the processional vista.

Plate 7: Bernini: Baldachin, St Peter's, Rome (view from nave)

In the words of a contemporary commentator on Urban VIII's poem: *Per Aeneam praesignatus fuit Pontifex Romanus . . . Verus iste Aeneas verus Rex Sacrorum est Romanus Pontifex* (Prefigured in Aeneas was the Roman Pontiff . . . The Roman Pontiff, true Aeneas, true king of the sacred rites).[2]

These prefigurations of the Pope in Aeneas, and of the papal *imperium* in ancient and imperial Rome, lift us into the realm of the timeless, and give added point to the hallowed formula, *Roma Aeterna*. The Baldachin over the Apostle's grave at the mid-point of St Peter's, taken along with the *Cathedra Petri*, together express the central point of that earthly portion of the cosmos which most adequately reflects the divine and the transcendent. In an essay on 'The Symbolism of the Centre' Mircea Eliade writes that "the very ancient conception of the temple as the *imago mundi*, the idea that the sanctuary reproduced the universe in its essence, passed into the religious architecture of Christian Europe: the basilica of the first centuries of our era, like the medieval cathedral, symbolically represents the celestial Jerusalem".[3] The hallowing of a piece of ground as a point of reference or centre is a fundamental act in the sacral apprehension of the cosmos. In primitive Roman religion this was the *mundus*; an area of the Palatine hill where a hole was dug into which corn was thrown, marking the juncture of the infernal and the terrestrial regions and serving as the central point on which the four basic directions of the city structure were orientated: east to west and north to south. The central *mundus* whence these measurements were taken was known as *Roma Quadrata*, and this system of fourfold orientation was basic to the structure of Italic cities, Roman camps and the interiors of Roman houses. It was a system modelled on what was conceived to be the general plan of the world as well as the four spatial zones of the cosmos. Such considerations throw an additional light on the symbolism of the Fountain of the Four Rivers, and endow Pythagorean factors with an atavistic base.

The fact that there are a plurality of 'centres' in primitive or religious cultures is no obstacle, for we are dealing with a mentality, as Eliade pointed out, where the centre is constituted by a hierophany or by ritual, a sacred geography that ministers to the innate religious instinct seeking a central space.[4] The aim is the restitution of a paradisal state or, as Christians would say, the condition of mankind before the Fall. The nostalgia for an earlier blessed time and place, for a Golden Age, is the product of a myth of wide provenance. The Romans had theirs, and a frequent theme in the exalted political propaganda of the great Augustan poets is the restoration by the Emperor Augustus of a state akin to the peaceful harmony of the *Saturnia Regna*. In Book VI of the *Aeneid* there is a passage redolent of a Rome providentially guided, when the dead Anchises unfolds to his son, Aeneas, a vision of Rome's future heroes, chief among them "Augustus Caesar, son of god, who shall set up the Golden Age where Saturn once reigned".[5] Then, in Book VIII, when Aeneas is conducted by King Evander around what was to be the future terrain of Republican and Imperial Rome, one is brought face to face with yet another kind of primal state: as they proceed, Evander shows Aeneas some of the sites which were to become the marble-clad majesty of Vergil's city, such as the Capitol, "which is now all gold, but was once wild and rugged, covered with woodland undergrowth". Approaching Evander's home, the home of a poor man, "they saw herds of cattle lowing everywhere about the sites of the Roman Forum, and the smart Carinae".[6] The mysterious beauty of Book VIII is among the most potent in the whole of the *Aeneid*, for it shows how Vergil's hyper-sophisticated imaginative powers still possessed an atavistic sense of sacred origins and a sacred centre: that centre, the Palatine and the Forum, whence though all vicissitudes the Republic and the Empire drew their mysterious strength and persistence.

Although the epithet '*Aeterna*' applied to Rome was not quite the commonplace in Vergil's Augustan period that it was later to become, when in the golden age of the Antonines Hadrian made it an official formula and instituted a cult in the Temple of Venus and Rome, the attitude which inspired it is already apparent in the first book of Vergil's *Aeneid*. There, in a famous passage Jupiter reassures Venus who is anxious about her son, Aeneas, the victim of Juno's anger, with the words, "for these [Romans to be] I set neither bounds nor periods of empire: dominion without end have I bestowed":

> *His ego nec metas rerum nec tempora pono,*
> *Imperium sine fine dedi.*[7]

That famous phrase, *imperium sine fine*, was later echoed by Dante at the climax of the *Purgatorio*, when, Vergil having departed, Dante is told by Beatrice that he is destined to be the citizen of another city, the city of God – *sarai meco sanze fine cive/ Di quella Roma onde Cristo è Romano*. By then all the turmoil and dissension of many centuries over Empire and Papacy, the Two Swords, Augustine's City of God and the City of this world, had intervened to give a context to that utterance of

Beatrice. That is to look ahead. In the centuries prior to the coalescence under Constantine the Great of the Catholic Church and the Roman Empire, the Empire itself seemed, in the eyes of its pagan beneficiaries, to bear a resemblance to the Ideal City, and to reflect in the regularity and stability of its imperial procedures something of the self-sustaining nature of the ancient world's cosmic religion, part Stoic and part Platonic.

Some such idea underpins Cicero's discussion of the Roman state in his *Republic*, where he writes that "a state ought to be so firmly founded that it will live forever, hence, death is not natural for a state . . . there is some similarity between . . . the overthrow and destruction and extinction of a state and the decay and dissolution of the whole universe".[8] The idea emerges at full strength in the reign of Antoninus Pius, in the famous oration which Aelius Aristides, a Greek rhetorician, composed during a visit to Rome in AD 143, an era which the neo-pagan Gibbon was later to celebrate as the peak of civilised order in world history. Aristides' visit took place during ceremonies to celebrate the birthday of Rome and the completion of the Temple of Venus and Rome, begun under the Emperor Hadrian and intended to symbolise the refoundation of the city, the renovation of the world, and the *saeculum aureum*. (Aelius Aristides' words may remind us of the end of Book VIII of Vergil's *Aeneid* where, portrayed on the shield wrought for Aeneas by his mother, Venus, a variety of peoples parade before Augustus Caesar, victor, pacifier and terrestrial cosmocrator). Aristides writes:

> Neither the Chelidonean nor the Cyanean promontories limit your Empire, nor does the distance from which a horseman can reach the sea in one day, nor do you reign

within fixed boundaries, nor does another dictate to you to
what point your control reaches; but the sea like a girdle
lies extended, at once as the middle of the civilised world
and of your hegemony. Around it lie the great continents
greatly sloping . . . There has developed in your
constitution a single harmonious, all-embracing union.[9]

Noteworthy here is the idea of Rome as centre of the world which, like some skilled artist, it orders in a comprehensive harmony akin – so the editor of Aristides' oration convincingly maintains[10] – to the Platonic notion in the *Timaeus* of a cosmos coming into being through the creation of a good world-soul, capable of creating the world-body. Thus, in this famous pagan celebration of Rome, we find the notions of unity and harmony characteristic of the cosmic religions of the ancient world, some of which passed into medieval Christianity by way of Stoicism and neo-Platonism. We find too the notion of a 'centre' which concentrates and reflects that universal harmony and whose benefits it is providentially destined to communicate to the *oikumene*. This was a claim of the Roman *imperium* which was to be embraced by the Catholic Church in general and by the papacy in particular.

There is a classic and marvellous essay by Friedrich Klingner on *Rom Als Idee*, in which he sums up the pagan Roman belief that their city was a cosmic centre, in words that show how the Roman religion of cosmos and *imperium* could find a place in a Christian context:

What Aeneas, the whole of Roman history, and Augustus
guarantee and make victorious on earth, is nothing other

> *than the lordship of almighty God, the shaping of earthly*
> *things through the spiritual power which governs the world:*
> *measure and structure, wrested from chaotic forces that on*
> *all sides lurk within and threaten from without. That is the*
> *great mission in whose light the cruel history of Rome*
> *receives its consecration: Rome subjugates what is formless*
> *and thus ensures for all races law, order, sense and unity;*
> *she represents the Logos on earth. For that reason Rome*
> *shares in the eternity of the cosmos.*[11]

For Christians only God is eternal, and this fact was of course never overlooked by the apologists and early Fathers, who were nevertheless prone to see the Church as a baptised prolongation of the Empire which had fulfilled its providential rôle of creating the *Pax Romana* as a suitable setting for the incarnation of the Logos. Clement of Alexandria, Origen and particularly Eusebius in the East; Lactantius, St Ambrose and Prudentius in the West: all were in varying degrees affected. Prudentius wrote a famous poem 'Against Symmachus', one of the stalwarts of the pagan aristocracy who opposed Christianity. In a *cause célèbre* of the late 4th century Symmachus opposed a decision to remove the pagan Altar of Victory which stood in the Senate House, and before which incense was burned prior to meetings. Symmachus foresaw trouble for the Empire in the abandoning of its providential deities. St Ambrose opposed him and won his case in 384. In 403 Prudentius summed up the whole affair from the Christian point of view, but in doing so makes apparent how much he retained of the old imperial spirit:

God taught the nations everywhere to bow their heads under the same laws and become Romans . . . For the time of Christ's coming, be assured, was the way prepared which the general good will of peace among us had just built under the rule of Rome. For what room could there have been for God in a savage world and in human hearts at variance, each according to its different interest maintaining its own claims, as once things were? . . . The constitution of life become stable and a settled way of thought draws in God in the heart and subjects itself to one Lord. Come then, Almighty; here is a world in harmony; do Thou enter it.[12]

Eusebius, a Church historian, and court-theologian to Constantine the Great, had at an earlier stage displayed an even more imperial attitude, and saw in the Constantinian Church the realisation of that dream of universal and perpetual harmony which had been a *leit-motif* of Roman imperial ideology. The imperial theme is constantly emphasised by Eusebius – "the Emperor frames this earthly government according to the pattern of the divine original, feeling strength in its conformity with the monarchy of God . . . Our Emperor derives the source of his authority from above"[13] – and gives a foretaste of the tensions that would arise when the papacy became a contender for such supreme authority. The latter claim was effected by Pope Leo the Great in the course of the 5th century, when the temporal power of the Western Empire was in retreat and Charlemagne still in the future, and when the Papacy was first able to include within its apostolate something of the majesty of the old imperium: St Peter, the first Pope, the *princeps apostolorum*, was, on the basis of two key biblical texts, held to have endowed all succeeding Bishops of Rome with the supreme and universal authority delegated to him by Christ.

The Feast of St Peter and St Paul on 29 June is to this day a prime occasion for sensing the special sacredness of the Eternal City on account of its providential election as the centre whence the faith was to be disseminated. Pope Leo the Great chose one such feast day to preach a famous sermon. He began by enjoining the city to remember their own special martyrs, St Peter and St Paul, "the men though whom the gospel of Jesus Christ shone forth for you; and you, who were the mistress of error, were made the disciple of truth. They were your true fathers and your true shepherds, who established you far better and far more fortunately for incorporation in the heavenly Kingdom than those by whose zeal the first founding of your walls was undertaken". The reference is to the supplanting of Romulus and Remus by St Peter and St Paul – the replacement of fratricide by fraternity. Yet the very adducing of the contrast cannot but have conveyed a symmetry, a patterned continuity, to the listeners. The Pope proceeds to remind the Romans that they have been called a holy people because they dwell in a royal and holy city which, through being the sacred seat of the blessed St Peter, is the *caput orbis*; and in order that the effects of the ineffable divine favour be diffused throughout the world, divine providence had prepared the Roman Empire, so that many kingdoms should be united in one empire. Furthermore – and hear the papal claims which Leo was to affirm make their appearance for future centuries – "the blessed Peter, prince of the apostolic order, was sent by destiny to the (ruling place) of the Roman Empire, so that the light of truth which was to reveal the salvation of all nations could more efficaciously diffuse itself from the centre through the body of the whole world".[14] Another sermon of Pope Leo, this time delivered on the feast of the birth of St Peter, dwelt on the famous and familiar text of St Matthew: *Super hanc petram aedificabo ecclesiam meam et portae inferi non prevalabit adversus eam* (Upon this rock shall I build my church and the gates of hell shall not prevail against it). Thence he derived what future centuries would call the *plenitudo potestatis* – the fullness of power; and ended by quoting Christ's admonition to St Peter: *Pasce oves meas*, 'Feed my sheep'. [15]

Twelve hundred years later that text was to figure twice in the Baroque redecoration of St Peter's; it accompanied a carved scene in the portico of the basilica, and appeared again on the back of the *Cathedra Petri*, the bishop's chair traditionally assigned to St Peter and encased by Bernini in a refulgent bronze and gold throne, well fitted to such a potent relic. Papal rhetoric did not become any less imperial in those later centuries, and found a culmination in the writings of St Robert Bellarmine. In a work such as *De Summo Pontifice*, St Robert, who then dominated the Catholic ideological scene, delivered the post-Tridentine version of papal triumphalism in phrases which echo those of Pope Leo, even though they are a little qualified by the harsh realities of intervening events: "We claim that the Pope as Pope, although he does not have any temporal power purely and simply, nevertheless, with due authority and for the cause of spiritual well-being, has the power of disposing of the temporal concerns of all Christians".[16]

The truly royal splendours of the Baroque papacy had their distant origin in the centuries after Pope Leo the Great, influenced by the ritualistic magnificence of Byzantine court ceremonies. In the 14th century the triumphalist splendour would adopt the triple tiara, thus finalising in a single visual emblem the claims to sovereignty which had earlier been promulgated by the Donation of Constantine, that forged document in which Constantine the Great apparently entrusted Pope Sylvester and his successors with the secular dominion of the Western Empire. Throughout the Middle Ages this document added enormous weight to the papal claims for sovereignty over secular rulers, for it was not until the 15th century that it was unmasked by the Renaissance humanist, Lorenzo Valla. Another such apocryphal event which bears on our theme is a story in the *Mirabilia Urbis Romae*, the mid-12th century collection of edifying but largely implausible tales about miraculous happenings in Rome, which was part of the medieval appropriation of the myth of *Roma Aeterna*. The story concerns the chains of St Peter, which in the late 4th century the Christian Empress Eudoxa brought from Jerusalem to Rome. When Eudoxa arrived back in Rome the pagan festival in honour of Octavius Caesar's Egyptian victory over Cleopatra was taking place. Such a victory celebration was something which no pope had as yet been able to stop, but Eudoxa's appeal to the Senate and people proved irresistible, and the *Christianissima Imperatrix* had her way. A Feast was established, and St Peter's chains came to rest in the Church of San Pietro in Vincoli.[17] The symbolism of this story reminds us how even by the early Middle Ages a transference of sacred centrality from Jerusalem to Rome was taking place. There is a map of the 13th century where both cities feature at the centre, evidence at least of their parity in contemporary eyes.[18] By the time of the High Renaissance popes the transference was virtually complete, and the iconography of the Crossing of the new St

Peter's incorporated that transmitted centrality in the triumphal symbolism of the Baldachin over the grave of St Peter; a St Peter whom, in the words of the early 13th century Pope, Innocent III, "the city exults in having as a protector; through him she who was the head of error has been made the mistress of truth; and now for a long time she has been more powerfully excellent on account of the *magisterium* of the apostle than formerly she was on account of imperial sovereignty – to which *magisterium* the Roman Emperor himself knows that he is subject".[19]

There, a little more than a century after Canossa, that first major coup of papal triumphalism which brought the Emperor to his knees at the feet of Gregory VII – a scene memorialised in a carving by Bernini under the statue of Countess Matilda in the new St Peter's – Pope Innocent III can calmly iterate as accepted fact the subordination, in the terminology of the age, of the *regnum* to the *sacerdotium*. The Two Swords had effectively become one, in the words of Augustinus Triumphus, a major medieval exponent of papal supremacy; the *tota machina mundi* was single, therefore there could be but one *principatus*. The *regnum* and the *sacerdotium* were in fact considered by papal apologists to be but two sides of one Christian Commonwealth, of which the Pope was head. Such reasonings, developed over centuries, had a plausible relation to reality in the 11th, 12th and the early 13th centuries when Gregory VII and Innocent III gave them the stamp of a then colossal authority. Papal claims to temporal power came to a climax in 1300 with the Bull of Boniface VIII, *Unam Sanctam*, at just the time when the balance of power was beginning to tip against the papacy in favour of the newly burgeoning national states. Yet, however impractical, papal claims were to persist into the 17th century. They had become part of the ideology of a papacy in which obsession with harmonious unity – cosmological, metaphysical and theological – had taken root, and was to be reflected in the ideal of a single Christian Commonwealth with the Pope as its head. In other words, the papacy claimed the centralising rôle in the affairs of the globe which the Roman Empire had assumed in the *oikumene* of an earlier age.

For Dante, the contemporary of Boniface VIII, the Roman origins of the Church still had great force and relevance. This can be illustrated from a section near the beginning of Canto II of the *Inferno*, where Aeneas figures in very much the same way he was to do for Bernini's Urban VIII, and for Innocent X, his successor, as *Pontifex Romanus per Aeneam praesignatus*[20] ("Since in the empyrean heaven he [Aeneas] was predestined to be father of gracious Rome and her Empire; both, in truth, being ordained the sacred place where sits great Peter's successor.")

Despite such a passage, however, it was evident to Dante that under the contemporary papacies of Nicholas III, Boniface VIII and Clement V the city, "to which after so many triumphs and glories Christ by word and deed confirmed the empire of the world",[21] had become embroiled in venal and worldly pursuits; he consigned all three popes to his *Inferno*. In his political treatise, *Monarchia*, he advocated the independence, under God, of the secular sword, and looked with hope to a resurgence of the Holy Roman Empire under the German Emperor, Henry VII. This was to prove a vain hope.

In certain other respects, Dante's vision of the Church was much closer to that of St Augustine in *The City of God* than to the theocratic tradition which we have been considering. Although

Augustine shared the common view of Rome's necessary rôle as the setting for Christianity, he had a reserved and even grudging attitude toward the Empire and, unlike men such as St Ambrose or Prudentius, had an ambiguous rôle in the history of Rome-centred ecclesiastical triumphalism. In his view there were two cities, one of this world and the Devil; the other of God, mingling in this world, in part leavening it, but working toward the building up of that eternal and invisible City beyond time, whose predestined citizens – "by grace a pilgrim below, by grace a citizen above" – cannot be known or numbered, and are not confined to the visible and institutional Church. Thus despite his reputation through the Middle Ages and beyond as a bulwark of theocracy and the authority of the visible Church, Augustine's views are full of ambivalence and cannot be captured in a formula.

So too with Dante. Yet while his most crucial allegiance was to that invisible city of God which is laid up in the eternal, there nevertheless breathes through the *Divine Comedy* a profound and complex attachment to Rome. It is surely significant that when Dante at the climax of the *Purgatorio* is told by Beatrice that he is intended by God to stay only for a short time in the Earthly Paradise at the top of Mount Purgatory, where in a visionary pageant all the central mysteries of Christian revelation are revealed to him, he is consoled by her in the following terms:

> *Qui sarai tu poco tempo silvano;*
> *e sarai meco sanze fine cive*
> *di quella Roma onde Christo è romano*
> (Here briefly you shall be a visitor. Thereafter,
> With me, you will be – unendingly – a citizen of
> That Rome where Christ himself is Roman).[22]

These mysterious lines vibrate in the memory of anyone attuned to the intertwining destinies of Rome and Christianity. In them Dante pays the eternal city of God the highest compliment he can: in it Christ will be a Roman, the one and only true Roman. Such was the potency of the one and indivisible, Christian, Catholic – and Roman – heritage.

The closing years of Dante's life coincided with the beginning of the Avignon exile of the popes, that eighty-year period when the papacy could no longer claim to be the visible legatee of *Romanitas*. The city lapsed into poverty, squalor and aristocratic factionalism, broken only by the tragic farce of Cola di Rienzo's régime. During his brief span of glory in mid-14th century he re-proclaimed the city as *Caput Orbis*, in the name of all its citizens: Cola being a Tribune of the People who eerily prefigured plebeian tyrants of the 20th century. There followed at the turn of the 15th century the Great Schism, which put even further into abeyance the equation Pope = Rome = Christendom. The first part of the 15th century, the Conciliar period, debated the desirability of vesting supreme authority in a General Council of the church, and questioned the supremacy of the papal office. Nicholas of Cusa eventually emerged as one of the champions of supremacy vindicated. The Popes returned to Rome. With the conscious intention of again making the city the focal point of Christendom, Nicholas V, the first truly Renaissance pope, who reigned from 1447 to 1455, planned a rebuilding of Rome, beginning in the Vatican area and including a new St Peter's. In the late 15th and early 16th centuries these apostolic ambitions reached a climax with that most imperial of Popes, Julius II, whose profiled countenance in all its arrogant humility can be seen in the Raphael fresco of the Mass of Bolsena in the Vatican *Stanze*. Julius had, as theologian and preacher at his court, Giles of Viterbo, General of the Augustinian Order – to which Luther belonged. A strong proponent of Roman and papal supremacy as well as the author of works blending Christian neo-Platonism with the Cabbala, Giles's writings contain some of the most ardent of all eulogies on the *Roma Aeterna* theme as perpetuated in the Church of Rome. Giles was specially stimulated by the expanding global horizons of the early 16th century, and even compared Pope Julius to Julius Caesar – to the latter's disadvantage: whereas Caesar only thought himself the ruler of the whole world, the present Julius could truly reign supreme by virtue of the discoveries in the New World of the Americas, and in the East. In 1507 Giles wrote an elaborate panegyric of the Portuguese voyages under the guidance of King Manuel I, entitled 'Fulfilment of the Christian Golden Age under Pope Julius II', which he delivered to the Vatican court.

Many of the themes that have occupied us in this chapter emerge in Giles of Viterbo's writings, but the context in which he was writing had changed. The medieval belief in a unified, harmonious and providentially ordered cosmos remained a force to be reckoned with, and papal claims continued to find strength along pseudo-Dionysian lines, since in the ordered hierarchy derived from the single divine Cosmocrator there was need for one supreme authority in the ecclesiastical realm. The whole neo-Platonic Christian tradition was, however, now under threat. The metaphysical *tabula rasa* of the Nominalist theologians – who influenced Luther – voided the participated glory of all elements of the cosmic harmony. The Protestant reformers decapitated the organic unity of the visible Church centred in Rome. Spurred on, however, by difficulties which were not recognised as terminal, the amalgam of neo-Platonic Christianity, scholasticism revived, and Roman papal triumphalism was about to manifest itself with spectacular wilfulness. Giles of Viterbo was thus the voice of a Church under threat, but a Church which was to emerge seemingly triumphant from the trials of the Reformation and the various Protestant heresies and apostasies. His had been a crucial voice ensuring that the themes which have exercised us in this chapter survived into the period of the Baroque papacy. The eminent Jesuit ecclesiastical historian, John O'Malley, has this to say:

> *Giles delights in contrasting Rome and the Vatican with Jerusalem and Sion. Without compromising the authentic character of the "old church of the Hebrews", he regards the Roman Church as the transcendent fulfilment of all that was imperfect and incomplete in the "Synagogue". In like manner Rome surpasses Jerusalem in spiritual excellence, and the hill of the Vatican becomes the true Mount Sion. What was essential to the "first Church" was its transitoriness, but what is most proper to the Roman or Vatican Church is that it will endure to the end of time. This could not be more graphically proved than by the fact that Solomon's Temple did not last even to the end of the eighth age of the old dispensation, whereas the eternal Temple of the New Law on the hill of the Vatican is even now rising to new magnificence. Rome is the holy city par excellence and the final focal point of history. It is, in a word, the holy Latin Jerusalem, "sancta Latina Jerusalem."*

> Reminiscent of the theory of the translation of the
> empire is the idea that the church migrated out of Asia into
> Europe, from Jerusalem to Rome . . . The transfer of the
> seat of religion from Jerusalem to Rome was absolutely
> necessary because of the universal character of the new
> religion. The church could not rest satisfied within the
> narrow confines of "Asia", but had to insert itself into the
> empire, the great universal institution of antiquity. Giles
> thus placed in the first generation of Christianity the seed of
> the eschatological hope for the religious unity of the human
> race, and he joined this hope indissolubly with the destiny
> of the city of Rome.[23]

We recognise from those last sentences how prominent is the
notion of Rome as centre of an all-embracing Catholic unification
of Christianity surviving the tribulations of the 16th century. The
Roman aspect of Catholicism gained yet further impetus from the
apostolic urge of the Jesuits, with their singular devotion to the
Pope; and it was furthered as well by all the other missionaries
whose activities were later centralised through the office *De
Propaganda Fide*, which was founded on Epiphany Day in 1622.
Prominent in devising a chapel for the college in 1634 was
Cardinal Antonio Barberini, Urban VIII's brother, one of the many
relatives whose career the Pope had advanced. The chapel was
designed by Bernini, the favourite of all Barberinis, though it was
later to be done over by Borromini. Called the chapel of I Re
Magi, and dedicated to the three wise men from the East, the
chapel was meant to symbolise, very suitably for the *Collegio De
Propaganda Fide*, the first accession to the infant Church of pagan

souls. On the Feast of the Epiphany there were always speeches by the students of the College in an immense variety of languages and dialects, Western and Eastern, in order to bring home the fact that the church was founded with a providential mission to encompass the diversity of the *oikumene*.

Plate 8: Bernini: Baldachin, St Peter's, Rome.

A modern parallel would be the different languages which the Pope uses to convey his greetings, *urbi et orbe*, in St Peter's Square each Christmas Day. On these occasions the Pope speaks from a balcony located over the main door of St Peter's, and thus centred above Bernini's gigantic colonnade, which extends its arms to either side of the square in a welcoming yet imperious embrace: "The ancient Roman formula – the imperial sun-symbol with religious coloration prefiguring pontifical glory, the radiating roads, the columns set up around the centre of the world – was to take on new life in the thought of Bernini".[24] Bernini, whose imaginative powers were well attuned to the Church's sense of her role, origin and destiny at that stage of her evolution, gave to St Peter's, the seat of the *Princeps Apostolorum*, to whom each Pope is deemed direct successor, its culminating and enduring visual impress. His buildings and statues speak the language of *imperium*, and his art has a conscious magnetism designed to gather up everything within its field of attraction.

Entering the great portico of the basilica, we pass beneath the carving of *Pasce oves meas* (Feed my sheep), push aside those tough, heavy leather pads at the doorway – always an enviable moment – and our gaze is at once taken in thrall by the distant Baldachin in all its swart, glittering immensity: nebulous, visionary, overmastering. Slowly the component parts assert themselves as we are drawn closer: the four darkly muscular bronze columns twisted in shape on the model of those in the temple of Solomon at Jerusalem, scrolled by branches of olive and conjoined by the tent-like flaps of a gold-emblazoned pelmet. At the top, four towering angels, ephebes of that assured and imperious gracefulness which is Bernini's way with angels, stand guard over the gilded, grey and rose spaces of the basilica, like so many winged victories; grave groups of *putti* interspersed between the angels support the emblems of papal power. Four huge volutes surge grandly upward behind the angels to an orb poised at their centre. At the base of the orb are attendant Barberini bees; atop is the cross of Christ. Way down beneath all this bizarre gigantism, to which the centuries have granted the gift of inevitability, is a relatively simple altar, at which the Pope alone may celebrate the sacrifice of the Mass, thereby timelessly re-enacting the Passion of Christ. Directly above that altar, blazoned forth on high in mosaic lettering around the inside of the dome is the key text on which the Church has always based its claim for a continuation in the office of the papacy of the authority with which Christ invested St Peter, *Tu es Petrus et super hanc petram aedificabo ecclesiam meam et tibi dabo claves regni coelorum* (Thou art Peter and on this rock I shall build my Church and I shall give to you the keys of the Kingdom of heaven): words inescapable to the view of anyone who, standing at the crossing next to the Baldachin and its altar, lifts his eyes above – as all are sure to do.

Flanking this sacrificial centre are four figures set in the niches of the colossal piers of the crossing: St Andrew, St Longinus, St Veronica and St Helena. All these figures are associated with relics of the Passion of Our Lord: the precious blood – Saints Longinus and Andrew; the sudarium – Saint Veronica; and a portion of the true cross – St Helena, the mother of Constantine the Great, who had brought it from Jerusalem in the 4th century AD. This last, which had been kept for centuries in the Roman Church of Santa Croce in Gerusalemme, was transferred by Urban VIII to the pier-niche at the Crossing. By taking such a relic to St Peter's, Urban VIII effectively ensured that St Peter's, and Catholic Rome, would be seen as the true reflection of the New Jerusalem, and the sacred centre of the cosmos. Thus Irving Lavin can write that, "For Bernini the Crossing of St Peter's had a specific topographical meaning. Both in a real and a figurative sense it was

Plate 9: *Bernini:* Cathedra Petri, *as viewed from the Baldachin, St Peter's, Rome*

Jerusalem, the place where salvation was achieved and is continually renewed. This ultimately is the meaning of the Baldachin and its crown and of the figures on the piers. The women concentrate upon the Passion and the sacrifice at the altar, the men upon the resurrection and redemption above, as if at the very time and place that the events occurred".[25] Thus viewed, the Crossing symbolises time's virtual abolition as it fuses with the transcendent, an effect intended by religious ritual in all times and at all places. Such an intersection of time and eternity was also the deepest intimation of neo-Platonism, through the temporal transfusing the eternal.

The Baldachin, an originally temporary structure held over Popes who were carried in state through the basilica, achieved its stasis in bronze; yet in Bernini's total ensemble it retains enough of its temporary and improvisatory nature to direct one's gaze through and beyond its giant ribs to the High Altar and the *Cathedra Petri*. There, at the culminating point of the great basilica, Bernini's genius gives visual expression to both the Roman and the Christian neo-Platonic themes that have been pursued throughout this book.

The focus of the great folds of gilt-bronze mantling and the four agitated supporting figures is an empty throne: the *Cathedra Petri*. In the ancient Orient as well as in Greece and Rome an empty throne was a symbol of supreme power which indicated the ideal presence of the ruler. Adapted to a Christian use, it is the throne of God that we see encased in Bernini's bronze; but it is also the original Bishop's chair of St Peter, and thus a sign that St Peter remains perpetually present in heaven to his Church, and that the Church is, so to speak, vertically open to the influxes of divine glory. Thus Fr Paolo Segneri, one of the preachers of the Roman Baroque, could deliver a panegyric on the *Cathedra* entitled: *Il Trono di Dio fra gli uomini collocato nel Vaticano* (The throne of God among men, situated in the Vatican).

The union of the celestial with the earthly – a great Baroque theme – is testified by the presence in the window above the *Cathedra* of the painted dove. This symbol of the Holy Spirit is the central point from which emanates a *Gloria* of angels and brilliant light. The *Cathedra* almost appears to levitate between the lower

Plate 10: Bernini: Cathedra Petri, *surmounted by dove and 'Gloria', St Peter's, Rome.*

and upper levels of the composition, as it is supported in only the most delicate, tangential way by the four Doctors of the universal Church, who, engaged as it were in some ecstatic *sacra conversazione*, flank the chair at the lower level. In the poses of the four doctors vis-à-vis the *Cathedra* there is nevertheless something that hints at their being bearers of a *sedes gestatoria*, and makes us dwell, too, on the even older *sella curialis* in which the highest officers of state were carried aloft in ancient Rome. That pagan overtone is reinforced by the triumphal palm-branches which curve out from the chair to pass behind two attendant guardian angels in poses of celestial nonchalance; and by the two little winged genii perched at the top of the empty throne who hold aloft the triple tiara and St Peter's Keys. Carved on the back of the chair itself, however, is the unequivocally New Testament scene of Christ's injunction to St Peter, *Pasce oves meas.*

The four ecstatic Doctors of the Church who figure below the *Cathedra* – St Ambrose and St Augustine of the Western Church in front, and behind, from the Eastern church, St Athanasius and St John Chrysostom – were all prominent figures in the discerning and rooting out of heresy during that crucial 4th century when the church was consolidating its primary dogma; furthermore, both Eastern Doctors had, most significantly, supported Rome's claims to primacy and universality. Their presence in such a prominent position would surely have had great resonance for the Church of the early 17th century, again so beset with heresies, and again so seemingly triumphant; if not in Europe itself, at least in the uttermost four corners of the globe. These were years when it must have seemed as if the desire of that 5th century Pope, St Leo the

Great, who had inherited so much of the spirit of the Roman *imperium*, and who first gave consolidated definitions of papal supremacy, was on the verge of being fulfilled: *"Primarius universalis Ecclesiae Pastor sedem haberet . . . ut Lux veritatis, quae in omnium gentium revelabatur salutem efficacius se ab ipso capite per totum mundi corpus effunderet"* ("The supreme shepherd of the Universal Church having his seat [here] . . . so that the light of truth, which was being revealed for the salvation of all peoples, might diffuse itself more effectively from this very head and centre throughout the whole world").[26]

Lux veritatis: the ancient symbol of the divine source of all being, so sympathetic to Christian neo-Platonism, finds brilliant visual expression above the *Cathedra Petri*. Except in times of darkness or thick cloud, the dove homing into the basilica through the oval window in the apse does so in a dazzle of natural light, which quickly breaks up into a golden blaze of spear-like rays, clouds, angels and putti – a heavenly brew which monumentally huge grey pilasters struggle imperfectly to contain. Clouds and rays then extend downwards to surround St Peter's chair and brilliantly illumine the tall gold mitres of the two foremost Doctors, whose balletic postures bridge the space between earth and heaven. Such is the imaginative control exercised by Bernini that the whole pulsating image is a perfect icon of unity, harmony and light, of emanation and return: the uncharted lapse of time gathered up into an 'artifice of eternity'. All is centred in Rome, in the basilica dedicated to the Prince of the Apostles, the inheritor of a Roman *imperium* sublimated into the world-wide *oikumene* of Catholic Christianity.

There is a passage of Hans Kauffmann that – concluding as it does on a quotation from Athanasius Kircher – gathers together splendidly so many of the themes which have thus far occupied us that it is worth quoting at some length:

Countless are the instances in which St Peter is characterised as a light-bringer, as well as compared to and identified with the sun. The sun-image contains within itself his uniqueness and his ubiquity. The supreme city of the earth obtained from him the light of the gospel, and he sent preachers into all lands. Like rays from the sun, like a river form its source the Christian religion has streamed out dazzlingly and world-wide from the Cathedra Petri. *Beginning its course in Jerusalem, it was as it were the rising sun which the Apostle at Antioch, the metropolis of the East, bequeathed to the whole earth; in Rome it was the sun at its mid-day zenith: shining forth over the whole world with the teaching of the gospel and banishing the darkness of error . . . [these images] lead us back to the* Cathedra. *Bernini's grandiose composition reflects such notions. The sun stands at its midday height. We shall only truly understand how heaven and earth intertwine like a vision of transfiguration if we are aware of the concept of Christocentrism. The* Cathedra *itself is not the centre, let alone the central light – that light rather stands above it . . . The radiance of that circle of light is incorporated into the* Cathedra – *the* Cathedra *comes near to the centre, reached closer than anything earthly to the source of light, but is nevertheless second in order, even though the nearest to it.* "Deus itaque Lux est . . . Spiritus ille amoris a Patre et Filio aeterna origine procedens . . . ex ineffabili Divinae Lucis fonte velute actinobolismi profluentes" – *Athanasius Kircher expressed it thus in his* Ars Magna Lucis et Umbrae (God therefore is light . . . That spirit of love proceeding from Father and Son as from a timeless source . . . flowing forth as it were like radiating shafts from the ineffable fount of divine illumination.)[27]

The stupendous edifice of St Peter's, finding its apotheosis in the two sublime *concetti* which Bernini devoted to the Prince of the Apostles, sums up a tradition of neo-Platonic, 'Dionysian' Christianity which was cosmic and emanational as well as sacramental and incarnational. It epitomised a moment in European culture which was both climactic – and transitional. Those who, despite all its glories, have found something excessive and strained in Baroque culture – perhaps on account of those very glories – have never been wholly in the wrong. In the period of Bacon and Hobbes and Galileo, of Descartes, Gassendi and Mersenne, religious sentiment had lost that core of silence and assured restraint which it had at the beginning of the High Middle Ages, made visible in the figures of the Portail Royal at Chartres. Bernini – and in this he typifies a good deal of what we mean by the Baroque – for all his virtuoso realism of surface, depends for his effect on a conscious deployment of illusoriness. The surplus of gesture, the beguilement of the senses, the aesthetic totalitarianism of the Baroque betoken a flaw, an element of strain, within the inherited ideal of harmonious, timeless unity. The Baroque must engulf you – or all is lost:

If at times the Baroque church only reveals the secrets of its structure to the specialist, God always reveals himself to all in a single immediate and violent intuition. His glory bursts from the first altars of the nave as from the far end of the apse. The flame of divine love pursues each one of us without respite, like the passionate preaching words which Ignatius of Loyola and the Fathers of Trent flung at the reconquest of Christendom. The heretic, the lukewarm, the libertin cannot half hide themselves behind a pillar and dodge the imperious arguments and the flames of the Real Presence; they cannot debate, give moderate assent, choose their saint, their symbol, their dogma: everything is given to them – flung at them – in an indissoluble and flaming unity.[28]

Notes to Chapter III

1. A link between Pope Innocent X and the Vergilian connotations of this heraldic device are made explicit in a contemporary poem occasioned by Innocent's election to the papacy, and quoted in part in Rudolf Preimesberger's 'Pontifex Romanus per Aeneam Praesignatus'. *Römisches Jahrbuch für Kunstgeschichte* (16), 1975, 252

2. cf. R. Preimesberger, 'Pignus Imperii: In Beitrag zu Bernini's Aeneasgruppe', *Festschrift Wolfgang Fraunfels* ed. F. Piel and J. Traeger (Tübingen, 1977) 320. cf. also Hans Kauffmann, *Bernini: Die Figürlichen Kompositionen.* (Gebr. Mann Verlag GmbH & Co.KG, Berlin, 1970) 37

3. M. Eliade, *Cosmos and History* (Harper Torch Books, 1959) 17

4. M. Eliade, 'Psychologie et Histoire des Religions – à propos du Symbolisme du "Centre"', *Eranos Jahrbuch*, Band XIX, 1950, 280-1

5. Vergil, *Aeneid*, VI, 792-4

6. Vergil, *Aeneid* VIII, 347-8 . . . 360-1

7. Vergil, *Aeneid*, I, 277-8

8. *The Republic*, III (34)

9. J.H. Oliver, 'The Ruling Power', *Transactions of the American Philosophical Society*, New Series, Volume 43 (4) 1953 (Sections 10 – 11 . . . 66)

10. J.H. Oliver, op. cit., 875-6

11. 'Roms Als Idee', *Antike* 29, 1927

12. Prudentius, 'Contra Symmachum' 11. 602 . . . 636 [Loeb Classics translation]

13. Quoted in C.N. Cochrane, *Christianity and Classical Culture* (OUP 1957) 185-6

14. St Leo the Great, *Sermon LXXXII* (Migne, P.L. LIV)

15. *Sermon LXXXIII*, ibid

16. St Robert Bellarmine, *De Romano Pontifice* V (vi)

17. cf. Robert Brentano, *Rome Before Avignon*, (Longman, 1974)

18. Illustrated and discussed in W. Müller, *Die Heilige Stadt* (Stuttgart, 1961) 111

19. Pope Innocent III, *Sermon* XXI (Migne, PL, CCXVII)

20. cf. note 2 above

21. Dante, *Epistle VIII*, 'To the Italian Cardinals'

22. Dante, *Purgatorio*, Canto XXXII, 100-103

23. J. O'Malley, *Giles of Viterbo on Church and Reform* (Leiden, 1968) 122-3

24. Yves Bonnefoy, *Rome 1630* (Flammarion, 1970) 42

25. Irving Lavin, *Bernini and the Crossing of St Peter's* (New York University Press, 1968) 35

26. Quoted in H. Kauffmann, op. cit., 271

27. H. Kauffmann, op. cit., 274-5

28. Pierre Charpentrat, 'Remarques sur la Structure de l'Espace Baroque', *Nouvelle Revue Française*, August, 1961, 219-220

CHAPTER IV

THE
BAROQUE
MOMENT

In the apse of St Peter's, to the right of the *Cathedra Petri* and opposite Giacomo della Porta's Renaissance tomb of Pope Paul III, Farnese, stands Bernini's tomb of Pope Urban VIII, Barberini. The support of the Barberini pope – endorsed, at first reluctantly, by his successor, Innocent X, and then by Alexander VII – had over a period of thirty years enabled Bernini to adorn Rome, the *Sancta Latina Jerusalem*, with overweening images of sacred splendour, thus exalting the pious, swamping the sceptical, and defying the heretical.

Bernini, prototype of the heroic individual of genius, as well as piously Catholic in the Jesuit-Baroque mode of his period, perpetuated the Renaissance tradition that the artist was the instrument of timelessness; and, as such, was eagerly courted alike by prince and by pope. In Petrarch's *Trionfi*, the 14th century prelude to Renaissance themes of death, fame, time and immortality, the Triumph of Death was capped by the Triumph of Fame, the latter a prefiguration of heavenly reward. The Triumph of Fame, however, was in turn followed by the Triumph of Time. Such intertwining paradoxes were to appear in Bernini's monument to Urban VIII.

It was in Christian tomb-sculpture of the 15th century that the impulse appeared to build monuments that were not just a record of mortality crowned by hope, but a testimonial of virtuous fame.

Pollaiuolo's recumbent Pope Sixtus IV, in the Grotte Vaticane, has the future felicity of his soul endorsed by attendant effigies of virtues and the liberal arts. By all accounts Michelangelo's blueprint for the tomb of Pope Julius II, intended for the new St Peter's but never brought to completion, was of a similar kind, only far more colossal, "fusing", according to Panofsky, "the influence of Roman sarcophagi with that of Pollaiuolo's tomb of Sixtus IV – and possibly with that of the triumphal arch scheme . . . It was dominated by the wish to glorify the Pope as a kind of Pantocrator and as a man who had succeeded in harmonising the threefold antithesis between the Old Testament and the New, between the Classical and the Christian ideals of human conduct (achieving, in Ficino's words, a *Concordantia Mosis et Platonis*) and, finally, between this life and the next".[1] Of that intricate and awesome structure the most famous segment remaining is Michelangelo's Moses, its brooding *terribilità* dwarfing a cramped setting in the Roman church of San Pietro in Vincoli.

What Julius II had missed Urban VIII was determined to achieve. From an early stage in his reign, when Venetian observers had noted in him "a hunger for glory" and a determination to follow any course "which could raise his name in opinion and make it famous in the future",[2] he took a keen interest in the construction of the tomb that would proclaim to the world both his mortality and his devout gloriousness.

Plate 11: Bernini: Tomb of Urban VIII, St Peters, Rome

123

The Pope, his hieratic countenance surmounted by the triple tiara, his seated pose a formidable mixture of blessing and admonition, with right arm extended in an imperious diagonal that lifts his mantle in a grandly encompassing fold, is a figure who guards and protects but above all commands. Here is authority incarnate, akin to the Marcus Aurelius statue on the Capitol, to God the Father with the mien of a Jove in Raphael's Chigi Chapel, akin even to Michelangelo's God the Father on the Sistine vault. The Pope, as apex of a triangular composition, is flanked beneath by virtues, Charity and Justice, which characterise him as Vicar of Christ. Of gleaming white marble, these figures are distinct from the sombre refulgent bronze of the rest of the monument. Charity is a female figure with that countenance of radiant wholesomeness which was clearly Bernini's predilection. Justice, intriguingly relaxed, has something curiously melancholy in her expression and pose. Could it be to show that the Pope exercises his authority in the sphere of Justice more in sorrow than in anger? At any rate, it is a figure that destabilises conventional response. Dwarfed by the Pope imperially throned above him, as well as by the Virtues to either side, the shrouded form of Death is absorbed in dutiful scribe-like fashion with a volume, a Roll of Honour so to speak, in which he is inscribing Urban's name. That bat-like skeleton has been compared to an allegorical figure such as *Historia*, who memorialises for posterity the living fame of a hero;[3] also to Fame who, in the guise of death, immortalises "the pretemporal essence of the very being whose temporal life he has ended". The notion of secular greatness as that which eternises, a thoroughly pagan as well as Renaissance aspiration, is adapted to a Christian context where the achievement of good name in this life "is a guarantor of fame as well as salvation".[4] As Urban VIII had himself expressed it, in one of the poems which made him so prominent a Latinist of classical humanism, *Mors tamen atra nequit praeclarum extinguere nomen* (Yet black death cannot extinguish an illustrious name).[5] Another skeleton appears in St Peter's on Bernini's funeral monument to Pope Alexander VII.

Plate 12: Bernini: Tomb of Alexander VII, St Peter's, Rome

This Pope, bare-headed, with hands upraised in prayer, encircled by attendant personifications of Charity, Prudence, Justice, – and Truth, clasping her emblem the sun – is decisively different from the Pantocrator figure of Urban VIII. In this instance, the skeletal personification of death is a half-hidden tangle of osseous angularities whose right arm holds up the hour-glass of mortality, and at the same time raises aloft the weighty red jasper folds of a canopy draped over the door of death. This skeleton seems far more unambiguously a *memento mori* figure than the busy scribe on the tomb of Urban VIII, yet, as Panofsky points out, "raised with such emphasis, and placed on exactly the same level as the sun of Truth, the hourglass, familiar symbol of time and transience, here signifies not only the power that ends life but also the power that reveals truth. He participates, though so to speak by indirection, in a task of glorification and vindication".[6] The whole effigy is decisively in the realm of Christian theology, but still within hailing distance of the pagan tradition of virtuous fame immortalising the occupant of a tomb; an echo of *Roma Aeterna* thus persists in the memorial to a supreme pontiff whose office was the sanctified prolongation of the Roman *imperium*. The Pope, his figure surmounting the composition, is so placed that his posture of humble devotion is aureoled with the majestic and the triumphant. The effect, as Hans Kauffmann claimed, is of an apotheosis, in which humble virtue *triumphs* over mortality,[7] and eternity over time. The sophisticated iconographical accounts of the skeletons on the tombs of Urban VIII and Alexander VII, to be found in Panofsky and Kauffmann, stressing as they do the ambiguous interplay of pagan fame with Christian death, should not tempt one to ignore more usual connotations of dissolution and transience: "Baroque Rome was the city of nothingness".[8] The tomb of Cardinal Antonio Barberini, Urban VIII's austere monk-brother, is to be found in the Capuchin Church of Santa Maria della Concezione, well-known for its adjacent ossuary of monks' skulls and skeletons. On that tomb are carved the words: *Hic iacet pulvis, cines et nihil* (Here lie dust, ashes and nothing). Even of Urban VIII's very different tomb Emile Mâle has remarked that the page on which the skeleton has just inscribed the Pope's name "will soon yield place to another, where a new name will be read".[9] This observation, more conventional than those of Panofsky or Kauffmann, catches something more straightforwardly characteristic of the mortality-fever of Baroque culture.

Gryphius, the German Baroque poet whose works, with an admixture of fierce Teutonic gloom, extend and vary the late medieval obsession with death and decay that persists into the Baroque period, has some lines which are pertinent to Urban VIII's tomb. They also corroborate the response of Emile Mâle:

> *Die vor uns abgelegt des schwachen Leibes Kleid*
> *Und in das Todten-Buch der grossen Sterblikeit*
> *Längst eingeschriben sind sind uns aus Sinn und Hertzen.*
> *Gleich wie ein eitel Traum leicht aus der Acht hinfällt*
> *Und wie ein Strom verscheust/den keine Macht auffhält:*
> *So muß auch unser Nahm/Lob/Ehr und Ruhm verschwinden.* [10]

(Those who before us have sloughed off
this frail bodily raiment, and whose names are
long since inscribed in the deathly
volume of almighty mortality, are quite gone

127

from out our hearts and minds. Just as a vain
dream slips easily from awareness, and a stream
dwindles when nothing sustains it, so vanish name
and praise and honour and fame.)

These lines, grimly and traditionally acquiescent of mortality, go counter to any suggestion of an eternity of virtuous fame. Yet do not the tombs of Urban and Alexander hold in poise both attitudes? The complexity of response which the monuments invite is best accounted for by excluding neither. There is grandeur as well as degradation, glorious commemoration as well as "a handful of dust". Nor should one overlook the characteristic touch of irony that Bernini introduces into those skeletons. On the Alexander VII monument there is something satirical about the arm that supports the heavy jasper folds of the canopy and, with a gesture part furtive, part aggressive, brandishes the empty hour-glass. Our reaction to the predominating majesty of the monument is tinged with repulsion at this skeletal presence – but does not a certain wry amusement also have its place in our response? As Borges put it, "the Baroque is that style which deliberately exhausts (and tries to exhaust) its possibilities, and borders on its own caricature." So too with the skeleton-scribe on the Urban VIII monument: the bent and bony manikin, so carefully industrious in his inditing, has a macabre comicality that contributes its mite to the *mélange* of melancholy, solicitude and grandeur which the monument comprises. We are, let it not be forgotten, responding to a culture in which hyperbolic eloquence was regularly infiltrated by ingenious conceits: a culture where the element of play was omnipresent.

Plate 13: Bernini: Tomb of Alexander VII (detail)

Plate 14: Bernini: Tomb of Urban VIII (detail)

The element of consummate play – of superabundant difficulty overcome by transcendent ingenuity – infiltrates some of the most famous Baroque expressions of mystical faith. Take Bernini's St Teresa and her Angel, with his impending dart of love: erotic overtones, falsifying if too exclusively stressed by a post-Freudian age, are best seen – as John Bayley once pointed out[11] – as the effect of "having it both ways", spiritually and sensually, at which the most astute Baroque masters were so adept. Viewed thus, even Donne's Metaphysical conceits warrant their inclusion by continental (as opposed to English) critics within a comprehensive Baroque style. However, the ecstasy of Bernini's Saint Teresa, or of his Blessed Lodovica Albertoni, does not quite veil the latent strain, desperation even, in figures subject to the engulfing presence of the divine. So too with the portrait-bust of Gabriele Fonseca, possibly Bernini's most intrinsically moving piece of sculpture: gaze taut with devotion, one hand convulsively gripping a rosary, the other pressed hard into draperies restlessly astir.

Plate 15: Bernini: Bust of Gabriele Fonseca, San Lorenzo in Lucina, Rome

131

It is as if, at this 17th century phase of Catholic religious culture, the determination to fuse the heavenly and earthly, and thus perpetuate the transcendence-immanence paradox of Christian neo-Platonism, was bought at the cost of an ambiguity that courts tension – and embarrassment. Vehemently, impetuously, the onlooker is drawn into closest proximity with something disturbingly intimate. At the same time, the experience is rescued from downright embarrassment by the virtuoso flourishes of technique at play amidst a recalcitrant medium. Baroque 'play' was not, however, ultimately frivolous, though the frivolity of the Rococo lay not far distant from it. Any culture centred around a court and a privileged élite – and where was this more so than in 17th century Rome? – has a pervasive element of play, whereby complexities of feeling are held in poise by stylistic panache. Baroque culture, with its elaborate vocabulary of gesture and its cultivated ingenuity, was also held in equilibrium by confidence in the circumambient harmony of the divine and the eternal: the Christian neo-Platonic synthesis whose pedigree was traced in Chapter II. There was an ultimate stability behind earthly change and metamorphosis, behind what Bossuet called *"le théatre des changements et l'empire de la mort"*.[12] Though conscious of being poised over an abyss of dissolution, Baroque culture was not nihilistic in the post-modern Nietzschean vein, where the proclivity to playfulness has an air of leaden contrivance. The Baroque could be sincerely joyous and grand despite its accompanying sense of the void, and retained a pagan festiveness and vitality amid its Catholic devotion, "the acute awareness of capacious time for ever slipping by . . . the tomb forever waiting around the corner as a reminder that flesh is mortal and that man is dust: all this led not to the despair of pessimism but to an extraordinary capacity for living. Baroque man could live with disenchantment, gather rosebuds while the moment lasted, and appreciate the colourful masquerade of living."[13]

Theatrical performance, both as an expression of mankind's ontological status and as a living reality of virtuoso scenic display, was a natural metaphor for the age's sense of itself. Fleeting moments of time are seized upon in all their transient splendour. They are illusions. What is not? But they are all part of the *Gran Teatro del Mondo.* They are like Crashaw's *Bubble*:

Sum venti ingenium breve

Flos sum, scilicet, aeris,

Sidus scilicet aequoris;

Naturae jocus aureus,

Naturae vaga fabula,

Naturae breve somnium.

Nugarum decus & dolor; . . .

Sum blandum, petulans, vagum,

Pulchrum, purpureum, et decens,

Comptum, floridulum et recens,

Distinctum nivibus, rosis,

Undis, ignibus, aere,

Pictum, gemmeum, & aureum,

O sum, (scilicet, O nihil.)[14]

(I am the wind's fleeting spirit,

Flower of the air, too, surely am I,

Star of the sea:

133

Nature's golden wit,

Nature's roving tale,

Her fleeting dream.

A sad, yet glorious bauble,

Intricate, sweet, yet vain . . .

Winsome, wanton, wandering,

Glorious, gleaming, fair,

A fresh and flowery ornament,

Set off by snow and roses,

By waves, by flames, by air,

Painted, bejewelled, golden

I am. For sure: Nothing am I.)

Existence for the Baroque artist was, as Spitzer put it, "magnificent in its very nothingness."[15] Over against that nothingness the Baroque raised its catafalques of praise and vainglory. Indeed a catafalque was among the most potent expressions of its nature: the *castrum doloris*, a transient structure raised like some theatrical set in a great church, adorned with images of grief and emblems of mortality, glittering with candles, studded with extravagant eulogies of the deceased, a visual focus round which the tides of Baroque pulpit eloquence copiously expanded. On one such famous and stately occasion, Bossuet, in an *Oraison Funèbre* for Louis de Bourbon, formulated the essential paradox of Baroque culture in a magnificent culminating image: "Come see what little remains to us of such noble birth, such greatness, so much glory; cast your eyes on every side – there you will see all that piety and generosity can do to honour a hero: titles, inscriptions, vain vestiges of that which is no more: figures that seem to weep around a tomb, and fragile images which time carried away along with all the rest; columns which aspire to carry to the heavens the magnificent testimony of our nothingness".[16]

"The magnificent testimony of our nothingness" – it is phrasing that would surely have appealed to the great theorist of Baroque paradox and *agudeza*, the Spanish Jesuit, Baltasar Gracián, whose fame has survived mainly on account of *El Oraculo*, a cynical manual much admired by Schopenhauer, which advocates the presentation of a mask of utmost politic prudence in confronting the jungle of human nature. Gracián was also the author of one of the most famous allegorical novels of the 17th century, *El Criticón*, and his prose, an unceasing flow of elegant and ornate conceits, distils all the grandeur in disillusion of Baroque culture. His two young heroes, Andrenio, an *ingénu*, and Critilo, a civilised reasoner, are conducted through a variety of morally annihilating misadventures towards a final destination, Rome, symbol of the vanity of existence and the depredations of time. Moreover it is not just to Rome that Gracián leads his two heroes but, specifically, to Piazza Navona:

> They chanced to hit upon a square, where a great crowd was assembled; without doubt it would be Piazza Navona, where there were to be found numerous people divided into swarms of whisperers, each gazing at its coarse attractions. Believe me, all we mortals are like temerarious ropewalkers over the slender thread of a fragile existence, with this difference: that some fall today, others on the morrow. Above it, men construct great dwellings and great dreams, raise up high towers of wind and thereon base their hopes.[17]

135

At this point, with Rome's Piazza Navona become the starting point for Gracián's great threnody of *desangaño*, it is well to remind ourselves of what an ambiguous symbol the Eternal City had become in the historical memory of European culture. On the one hand, a site where the remains of pagan glory inspired the artists of the Renaissance and the Baroque to raise Christian temples and monuments that would make of modern Rome the New Jerusalem. On the other hand: Rome, the supreme and ultimate Theatre of Vanity. Not just a vanity of physical ruin and transience, but also of spiritual and moral vanity. Santillana, in his book, *The Crime of Galileo*, epitomises with stinging eloquence a complaint that has resounded down the centuries, and persists to this day:

> *We should try to think of the Rome of those times, where much saintly work was being done for the poor and the pilgrims from all parts of the world, where true saints could be found, to be sure, but which otherwise was the most corrupt of administrative capitals, and still and forever such as Du Bellay had found it a century earlier and as Belli was to portray it two centuries later: packed with fanatical and petulant monks, shrewd intriguers, postulants, paid and unpaid observers, diplomats, cynical secretaries, fulsome literati and inane versifiers living off the bounty of some prelate; lazy insolent nobles, curialist lawyers, stony-faced publicans rack-renting for the princes and the convents; spies, informers, go-betweens, men about town, unctuous priests and officials, careful hypocrites, suspicious hard old men, meeching young men on their way to preferments through oily conformism; all the parasitical, torpid, cunning,*

and malevolent society that vegetated like a pestilent mushroom growth on the fringes of an imperial world bureaucracy and for whom the stability and prestige of that bureaucracy in matters spiritual meant their career and their income. Around it all, the stones and the sky and the people of the Eternal City, expressing its spirit as it endures through time.[18]

The stones of the Eternal City – stones of those Roman edifices that are both objects of awe and provocations to despair – have inspired many a poet to elegise the vanities of aspiring glory. Du Bellay's *Ruins of Rome*, done into English by Edmund Spenser in the late 16th century, catches the recurrent strain of frowning eloquence:

Thou that at Rome astonisht dost behold
The antique pride, which menacèd the skie,
These haughtie heapes, these palaces of olde,
These wals, these arcks, these baths, these temples hie;
Judge by these ample ruines vew, the rest
The which iniurious time hath quite outworne,
Since of all workmen helde in reckning best,
Yet these olde fragments are for paternes borne:
Then also marke, how Rome from day to day,
Repayring her decayèd fashion,
Renewes herselfe with buildings rich and gay;
That one would iudge, that the Romaine Daemon
Doth yet himself with fatall hand enforce,
Againe on foote to reare her pouldred corse.[19]

'The antique pride, which menacèd the skie': The Tower of Babel allusion cannot be missed. In one of his last books, *Turris Babel*, Athanasius Kircher himself skirts round the hallowed theme of Rome as an emblem of *Vanitas* and hence as a derivative of Babel.

Plate 16: Athanasius Kircher, Turris Babel, *(Amsterdam, 1679)*

Almost certainly inspired by an engraving Kircher must have seen of the painting of Pieter Brueghel the Elder. The criss–crossing spiral effect of the gigantic pile is flanked at its base by a proliferation of smaller edifices, symbolising mankind's hubristic ambition to leave enduring monuments – beautiful nonetheless. The tower may well recall the spiral effect on the exterior of Borromini's cupola of San Ivo alla Sapienza.

Nimrod's wondrous but prideful construction provoked God to punish with a confusion of tongues, a punishment mitigated at Pentecost: the descent of the Holy Spirit upon the Apostles, endowing them on that occasion with the gift of tongues, proved susceptible down the Christian centuries of a pious gloss, whereby it became the anti-type of the Tower of Babel. The kind of ambition exemplified in the attempt to build the Tower was in its turn easily fused with the traditional topos of *Vanitas* of which pagan Rome was an instance; and that is what Kircher does in a section of *Turris Babel.* He was himself of course the servant of pontiffs who were not averse to erecting heraldic mementos of their own building feats, and he tactfully distinguished between buildings acceptable because they promoted a spiritual link with the heavens, and pride-induced Nimrodian structures: "And so let those ambitious of glory in the building of vain structures be mindful, if they wish to attain the weight of eternal glory, to labour at building churches in honour of God; let them devote their energies to creating hostels destined for the use of receiving poor pupils; let them build colleges for the young in which all virtuous arts can be cultivated. Those indeed are towers not of Nimrod, but the constructions of devout minds, whose pinnacles reach to the heavens, as it were preparing a ladder to the summit of eternal happiness . . . „[20]

In other passages of *Turris Babel* Kircher has less need to tread carefully and he handles the *Vanitas* theme in traditional Humanist fashion. Yet the very occurrence of Rome as *Vanitas*, in such an accredited *apparatchik* of the papal régime, adds a dimension to our grasp of Rome as City of Time as well as of Eternity:

Emulators of the Babylonians, being brought to Egypt, knew
no measure in erecting obelisks, pyramids, labyrinths. The
Greeks and Romans following them distinguished
themselves in the building of circuses, amphitheatres, baths,
aqueducts – to this day we wonder at them, half-buried as
they are in ruins. The deceit and uncertainty of our
temporal condition assures us of nothing firm, nothing solid
. . . They laboured at building towers whose height should
outsoar the heavens . . . What great palaces and pleasure
gardens we see constructed with every kind of extravagant
beauty . . . a hundred years go by and, transferred to other
and yet other families, all memory is lost of whose palaces,
whose villas they originally were. Such was the nature of
Nimrod's builders who . . . in place of glorious eternal
happiness, suffered total disaster.[21]

Thus are the glories of *Roma Aeterna* placed under the aegis of the
cohorts of Nimrod, chief architect of the Tower of Babel. Kircher,
in the endearing fashion of classical humanism, does not hesitate
to put into the mouth of Nimrod a lengthy imaginary speech, fiery
and proud, rather like one of Satan's in *Paradise Lost*, exhorting his
followers to more sterling constructive efforts. Kircher was
convinced that Nimrod, an historical personage for him, must have
been the greatest architect who ever lived, and describes not
without relish the planning, materials, and constructive techniques
of his tower:

Come, to work, let us dig out supplies of chalk and clay, let
us bake surfaces with fierce fire, let us dig and lay down

140

foundations according to this plan at long last devised by me, which explains the properties of each and every part of the work to be achieved. Be active, not idle; let us gird ourselves to the task.[22]

The architectural zeal of the Roman Baroque, made manifest willy-nilly in Kircher's imaginary version of Nimrod's speech, was of course subordinate in *Turris Babel* to a traditional moral: the building of the heaven-storming Tower was a symbol of pride, whereupon God destroyed the unity of sinful mankind by afflicting it with diversity of tongues. Even this punishment, however, is presented by Kircher almost as a Fortunate Fall, since God left man with his reason, will, memory, vocal organs, teeth, lips, tongue, breath, all intact: thereby he could master many languages and disseminate the eternal message of the Gospel through efforts of translation:

The Lord graciously gave a remedy: one should learn languages with reason as guide and mentor. This new grace poured forth, an inexhaustible fount of good, so that, by virtue of interpreted words, those joined together again who were long separated by that Babylonian confusion. This occurred most conveniently for the good of the Gospel, not by human devices, but by divine favour, whereby Moses, the fount of all wisdom, and the writings of the Hebrew prophets, did not only come via the seventy translators to the Greeks, but also through other translators of the Holy Scriptures came to the other, barbarous peoples, and today are read in the language of almost all peoples. We have reason, productive of works that truly are divine as well as human; we have concepts by means of which we investigate things and causes; we have a tongue – a most excellent organ if properly fitted to its task; we have pen and paper; with all these we shall piece together the wisdom of God, and we shall candidly receive what is opposed to us: for Christ in all things will abundantly suffice.[23]

The active optimistic spirit of the Jesuit sees all things turned to good: even the punishment of Babel was a stimulus to linguistic versatility and the further exercise of reason. This seemingly rather worldly moral is interwoven, however, with a more decisively Biblical and theological gloss, which had for many centuries been adduced for the Tower of Babel and had its source in the 4th century theological writings of Origen. The disjunction of tongues at Babel was compensated for later by the gift of tongues descending on the Apostles from the Holy Spirit at Pentecost – "in Jerusalem the world as it were contracted into one whole". This was the founding moment of the church's mission to evangelise the globe:

Christ the Lord abundantly filled with the Holy Spirit the gathering of the disciples. He will send them forth to the kings and peoples of all nations, not to found the things of Babel, or to capture for themselves kingdoms and empires, or labour and contrive against the knowledge of God, but to attract the whole world into confessing the Catholic faith, so that they may found a city of the true, living God, whose foundations and head and keystone and ruler is Christ the Lord of Glory – who commands the right way to go about this: not with hammers, scoops, plummets, axes and iron tools, not by swords, spears, lances or brazen weapons, but through the Holy Spirit, through knowledge of divine things, through holiness of life, through all manner of virtues, and through skill in languages.[24]

Implicit in that passage is the idea of the Church as the new Tower; the Tower of Divine Wisdom, not built with human hands but inspired by Christ the Logos and by the Holy Spirit. Just as the confusion of tongues at Babel was occasioned by the sin of man, and was followed by discord, ignorance and polytheism – the latter exhaustively charted by Kircher in later sections of *Turris Babel,* in the course of an eccentric account of linguistic history – so the first miraculous work of the Holy Spirit was a temporary suspension of that confusion, representing the inward harmony and mutual understanding of' believers. It was a symbol and prophetic intimation of' the new divine life among nations of all languages, and of the reception and absorption of all national peculiarities in the universal mission of the church. Its pertinence to the perfervid apostolic mood of the Jesuits and of other *Propaganda Fide* missions in the 17th century hardly needs to be stressed. Such a message was writ large and radiantly on the vault of the Jesuit Church of San Ignazio.

There is another Baroque church in Rome that conveys a similar message, not through the iconography of the four continents to be found in San Ignazio, but through the Tower of Babel and related Pentecostal themes: this is Borromini's San Ivo alla Sapienza, the church of the University of Rome. Built over a period of thirty years under the patronage of the three 'Baroque' popes of the mid-17th century, Urban VIII, Innocent X, and Alexander VII, San Ivo is embellished to a greater or lesser extent by the heraldic devices of each one of them: the Barberini bee is imaged in the hexagonal shape of the ground-plan; the Pamphili dove and the fleur-de-lis grace the exterior of the tower; and, most prominent of all, the eight-pointed star, the six *monti*, and oak-tree with its leaves and acorns of Pope Alexander VII, Chigi, generously embellish both exterior and interior. The Chigi emblem of the *monti* – oddly suggestive of the triple tiara – surmounted by the eight-pointed star, as well as being prominent on all four sides of the interior of the cupola, flank the frontal view of the exterior of the drum as well. Thence the eye ascends to the cupola, whose buttresses press inward toward the lantern, which in turn culminates in the extraordinary and unforgettable helical spiral. This 'ziggurat' effect, a Babylonian motif, surely adds plausibility to the view of those who, like Hans Ost, interpret the iconography of the Church in terms of the Tower of Babel-Pentecost paradox. Anthony Blunt, in his book on Borromini, has taken serious account of Ost's interpretation, along with several others, and summarises matters thus:

> *The similarity of the lantern of S. Ivo to the ancient ziggurats of Mesopotamia has often been pointed out, and it is more than likely that Borromini knew engravings, such as one by Martin van Heemskerk, which show the Tower of Babel in this form. By a curious twist, however, the tower, which started as a symbol of human folly, later came to be*

used to represent the exactly opposite idea, and the confusion of tongues associated with Babel was transformed into the knowledge of tongues given to the Apostles at Pentecost, as represented in the interior of the church. The Tower of Babel becomes the turris sapientiae, *the tower of wisdom, and was even used by Martin van Heemskerk to represent the light-giving pharos of Alexandria, an obvious symbol of wisdom. It also occurs as a symbol for the wisdom of Solomon in a fifteenth-century painting by Butinone (in the National Gallery of Scotland), in which the youthful Christ arguing with the doctors in the Temple is shown on a spiral structure like the lantern of S. Ivo.*

The top of the whole structure is composed of a series of symbols taken from the Iconologia *of Cesare Ripa, first published in 1593 (first illustrated edition 1603), and a favourite source for seventeenth-century artists. The wrought-iron, flame-like structure represents the desire for knowledge, inspired by intellect; and the flaming torches round the base of the lantern stand for knowledge itself.*[25]

The iconography of knowledge and wisdom, suitable for a University church, is prominent too on the interior of San Ivo, where Solomonic motifs, "figures of cherubims and palm-trees and open flowers" (I. Kings, 6, 29-32) proclaim its affinity with the Temple of Wisdom in the Old Testament. The six-pointed star, which alternates with the Chigi eight-pointed star, was itself a *Sigilla Solomonis* and, interesting to note, commented on as such by Kircher in his *Oedipus Aegyptiacus.*[26] Solomonic palm-trees

Plate 17: Borromini: Exterior of San Ivo alla Sapienza, Rome (detail)

twine with Chigi oak-leaves, thus establishing a link between Old Testament Wisdom – in Christian theology a type of the Logos as well as of the Holy Spirit – and the Pope. This is just such a conflation of Pope, Divine Wisdom and Holy Spirit as was seen in Sacchi's *Divina Sapienza* fresco in the Barberini Palace, beneath which Pope Urban VIII had sat to read a passage from the Book of Wisdom. An anonymous commentator took this to reveal Pope Urban as Wisdom Incarnate.[27] For another commentator, Tetius, it had Pentecostal overtones as well: ". . . minds forever flooded with such great light".[28]

In San Ivo the iconographical blend of Divine Wisdom with the papal office is part of a configuration that unambiguously incorporates Pentecostal imagery. At the very top of the inside of the lantern, flanked by twelve columns, is the dove, symbol of the Holy Spirit, enclosed by a sun-burst of flames. From the star-girt circular opening of the cupola beneath, twelve lines of alternating hexagonal and octagonal stars descend to the entablature, stopping directly above the twelve niches in the lower level of the church, which, in the original design, contained statues of the twelve apostles. Hans Ost interprets the lines of stars as analogous to Pentecostal flames, as found in San Marco in Venice, descending from the dove of the Holy Spirit to be the inspiration of the apostles at Pentecost. Ost's concluding section sums up the overall iconographical implications of San Ivo della Sapienza in a fascinating, if as yet partly speculative way:

As Sapientia Babilonica *the tower of the University Church is borne up by the twelve columns of the lantern, which correspond to the twelve columns of the interior*

Pentecostal programme; it is decorated with the flame-crown and precious stones which according to Tetius are associated with the papal house; and it is lighted by the flames and the candelabra which stand above the apostle-columns as Pentecostal fire of wisdom. The Tower of Babel has become the dwelling of God and of the papal Church, which announces true doctrine to all the world. The Jews in their exile by the waters of Babylon and then the exegetes of the Old Testament, were only able to see in the Tower of Babel an image of human pride; it was only later in Christian exegesis that the original meaning of the ancient oriental ziggurat was again established: one builds over against the heavens so that God can descend to the summit of the Temple-Tower, and then take up his dwelling amid populous cities. So in Rome, the new centre of the world, God is present in his representative, the Pope; the outpouring of the Holy Spirit and the Pentecostal miracle, which empower the Church to speak to all the peoples of the earth, here happen daily anew. Rome and its unity is the seat of Divine Wisdom. Borromini's University Church is not alone. The Triumph of Rome's teaching, expressed by Borromini in architecture, is likewise found in painting and sculpture: in Sacchi's fresco of Divine Wisdom and in Bernini's Cathedra Petri. *In all these monuments the divine appears on high in the clouds as the dwelling-place of papal wisdom; in all of them the* Magisterium *is placed under the sign of the Holy Spirit and a claim advanced over the whole globe.*[29]

Pentecost, along with the Incarnation itself, is the supreme instance of what T.S. Eliot called the "intersection of the Timeless with time". Not on the semi-pagan cosmological model of neo-Platonism, which sees time as an imperfect reflection of the timeless One, but as a direct influx of the Triune personal God into historical time as a providential process, thereby initiating the reintegration of that primordial unity whose loss was symbolised by the myth of the Tower of Babel. The Church becomes, as in the iconography suggested for San Ivo della Sapienza, the counterbalancing Tower of Wisdom, the link between heaven and earth.

Plate 18:

Borromini: Interior of San Ivo alla Sapienza, Rome (detail)

The Church is also, typologically speaking, the new Ark of Noah, which represents – once again Kircher has the relevant words – "the miracle of the world, the epitome of the geocosm, the seminary of the whole of living and sentient nature, the refuge of a world due to perish, and the happy and blessed augury of a world in process of being reborn".[30] Certain features of the Ark, in Kircher's fanciful but characteristically thorough account in another late work, *Arca Noe*, are in significant contrast to the maleficent suggestiveness of the Tower of Babel in its conventional signification as symbol of evil. These features are interestingly brought out by Valerio Rivosecchi:

> *On the architectural level the contrast between the wisdom of Noah and the sublime ignorance of Nimrod seems an exact antithesis of two archetypes: the rational anthropomorphic scale of the Ark, with its strict orthogonal structuring, as against the colossal, impossible and fantastic scale of the Tower, which swells with curving forms in illusory spaces. And naturally the contrast is reflected on the allegorical plane: the Ark in its simplicity leaves little room for imagination but much for the art of analogy, where it can be exercised in the smallest detail. The Tower, by contrast, has no analogical potential, offers no scope for an allegorical reading of single details, because in its form it shows an intuition of what actual mental movement is like; it is the image of a journey in which the mind can at each moment lose its equilibrium, it is the image of the tortuous convolutions achieved by the human intellect in its journey towards knowledge.[31]*

To Manfredo Tafuri, the 'Babelic' spiral does more than threaten a loss of equilibrium, it is a radically destabilising image. For him Borromini – whom he calls the *"negazione del gran' teatro del mondo"* – is an anarchic and undermining figure who heralds the rending asunder of the ideal of unity contained in both papal and imperial Rome. Tafuri, with somewhat idiosyncratic fervour, tracks variants of Borromini's 'Babelic' spiral in some of the prints of the 18th century Piranesi, where they form a small but far from insignificant feature.[32] He blends them with his own response to the vast fold-out plan of late imperial Rome in Piranesi's *Campus Martius* series, which symbolises on a far bigger scale the loss of wholeness and harmony which had been preserved throughout the Christian-Classical centuries and was epitomised by Rome as cosmic centre and 'Eternal City':

> *The City has become* inhospitable. *Useless to seek in it a true habitation, useless the attempt to extract from it a coherence. The clash of gigantic monads singing an atonal requiem for the pre-established harmony of Leibniz leaves open only tortuous and broken paths which penetrate laboriously amid the interstices of this "theatre of decomposition".*[33]

The phrase "theatre of decomposition" hardly does justice to Piranesi, but it does capture something of his intuition into the disrupted unity of European civilisation. Piranesi's powerful and disturbingly ambiguous images of Rome, which are the subject of the next chapter, record the Triumph of Time.

Notes to Chapter IV

1. E. Panofsky, *Tomb Sculpture* (Thames and Hudson 1964) 90

2. J. Hook, 'Urban VIII, the Paradox of a Spiritual Monarchy', *The Courts of Europe*, ed. A.G. Dickens (Thames and Hudson, 1977) 224

3. Hans Kauffmann, *G.L. Bernini, Die Figürlichen Kompositionen* (Berlin, 1970) 119

4. E. Panofsky, 'Mors Testimonium Vitae', *Studien Zur Toskanischen Kunst*, ed W. Lots (München, 1964) 222 . . . 230

5. Maphaei S.R.E., Card. nunc Urbani Papae VIII, *Poemata* (1640)

6. Panofsky, op. cit., 45

7. Kauffmann, op. cit., 326

8. P. Ariès, *The Hour of Our Death* (Penguin books, 1983) 345

9. E. Mâle, *L`Art Réligieux de la fin du XVIe Siècle, du VXIIe Siècle et du VXIIIe Siècle* (Paris, 1951) 220

10. Gryphius, 'Menschliches Elend', *Gedichte* (Reclam, 1968) 6

11. London Review of Books 9 (5) March, 1987; a review of B. Brophy's *Baroque 'n Roll*

12. J.-B. Bossuet, *Sermons* (II) (Garnier, Paris) 456

13. P. Skrine, *The Baroque* (Methuen & Co., 1978) 153-4

14. *The Poems, English, Latin and Greek of Richard Crashaw*, ed., L.C. Martin (Oxford, Clarendon Press, 1927) 219 . . . 220

15. L. Spitzer, *Essays on 17th Century French Literature* (CUP, 1983) 141

16. J.-B. Bossuet, *Oraisons Funèbres*, I (Editions Garnier) 214

17. B. Gracián, *El Criticón*, (Editorial Planeta, 1985) 562 . . . 564

18. G. de Santillana, *The Crime of Galileo* (Heinemann, 1958) 117

19. E. Spenser, *Poetical Works* (OUP 1952) 513

20. A. Kircher, *Turris Babel* (Amstelodami, 1679) 23

21. A. Kircher, ibid., 90-91 . . . 23

22. Kircher, ibid., 30

23. Kircher, ibid., 127 . . . 129

24. Kircher, ibid., 128-9

25. A. Blunt, *Borromini* (Allen Lane, 1979) 126

26. cf. P. de la Ruffinière du Prey, 'Solomonic symbolism in Borromini's Church of S. Ivo della Sapienza', in *Zeitschrift für Kunstgeschichte*, I (1968) 224

27. G. Incisa della Rochetta (*L'Arte*, Vol. XXVII (2-3) 64) quotes the contemporary passage

28. G. Tetius, *Aedes Barberinae* (Romae, 1642) 95-6

29. H. Ost, 'Borromini's Römische Universitätskirche San Ivo alla Sapienza' *Zeitschrift für Kunstgeschichte*, XX (1967) 133-5

30. A. Kircher, *Arca Noe* (Amstelodami, 1675) Dedica

31. V. Rivosecchi, *Esotismo a Roma Barocca* (Bulzone Editore 1982) 108-9

32. M. Tafuri, 'Borromini e Piranesi: La Città come "Ordine Infranto"', *Piranesi: tra Venezia e l'Europa*, a cura di E Bettagno (Firenze 1983) 89-90: (Tavola 12 della *Prima Parte de Architettura* (1743) . . . Mausoleo Antico nella tavola 3 della stesso volume . . . nella *Caduta di Fetonte;* nella tavola 7 della *Carceri;* nel secondo frontespizio della *Antichità Romane* . . .)

33. ibid., 95

CHAPTER V

TIME TRIUMPHANT:
PIRANESI
AND THE
ENLIGHTENMENT

"I need to produce great ideas, and I believe that were I given the planning of a new universe I would be mad enough to undertake it".[1] That has the true Promethean ring of the eighteenth century Sublime. In Piranesi's best evocations of Rome he could virtually be said to have fulfilled this ambition, since they transfigure the material and create a new universe of the imagination. Extravagant and sombre, Piranesi's vision adds fresh dimensions to our experience of space and time. Nowhere is the aspiring extravagance of Piranesi's imagination more evident than in the series of prints which he made of the Campus Martius, that section of Rome stretching roughly from the present-day Corso to the bend of the Tiber. In Piranesi's time it was as densely covered as it is today with Renaissance palazzi, Baroque churches, and dwelling places dating back to the Middle Ages. In Roman imperial times, too, it was extensively overbuilt. In his plates of the Campus Martius, however, Piranesi, like some demiurge revising its plan for the universe, has stripped away the accretions of subsequent ages and isolated the structures of Roman times in all their awesome mass. These ruins of the Campus Martius, like many other *Vedute*, in their crumbling grandiosity portend never-ending space:

> *Roman handling of space in major structures of the middle and late empire was, indeed, concerned with vast vaulted interiors that drew men, as it were, into gigantic shells from which prospects opened up into subordinate units in a succession of limited, if long, vistas. But in Piranesi's interpretation, these interiors become sections of an infinite space. In the magnificent late view of the Hall of the Great Baths in Hadrian's Villa, as in other mature ruin views, the broken walls and vaults do not seem to be the remnants of a self-sufficient spatial unit but of an infinite ensemble.* [2]

Space, so prominent in the visual extravaganzas of the Baroque, has ceased in Piranesi to suggest a distantly encompassing celestial realm. Whether it is defined by the interior of a building, a cavernous underground chamber or a receding colonnaded vista, space – along with time – had become the sole and native element of all that exists. "The Baroque cycle had come to its end. Its way had been from bodies to space, from space to chaos."[3] Humankind dwelt no more in a pre-ordained cosmos but in a medium without beginning or end, filled with colossal structures betokening Promethean will and defiance which, despite their Babylonian mass, are like the chaotic and corroded witnesses of some vanished dream. Even the *Ichnographia*, that enormous imaginative reconstruction of the ground-plan of Rome in the age of Constantine the Great which unfolds from the Campus Martius folio, in its entirety makes – and this despite the planimetric coherence of its parts – a nightmarish impression of de-centred proliferation:

> Not by accident does it take on the appearance of a homogeneous magnetic field jammed with objects having nothing to do with each other. Only with extreme effort is it possible to extract from the field well-defined typological structures. And even when we have established a casuistic complex of organisms based on triadic, polycentric, multilineal laws, or on virtuoso curvilinear layouts, we end up with a kind of typological negation, an "architectural banquet of nausea", a semantic void created by an excess of visual noise. [4]

The Promethean will of the godless Enlightenment and succeeding periods, in an excess of planned order paradoxically fell victim to nihilistic fragmentation, and aspired Babel-like to fill space with overweening memorials. Piranesi, who intended his Campus Martius experiments to inspire the architects of the modern age, was a portent. Yet, just as strong as the impression of aspiring mass in Piranesi's Rome is its desolation, the all-pervasive medium of time casting shadows of ruin and decay. Hence the curious double effect that Piranesi's works make, as colossal in melancholy as they are in energy:

> The man of the Enlightenment cuts his moorings with the
> absolute; against essence, he chooses existence, that is to
> say his own becoming, and proclaims himself sole maker
> and architect of his destiny. An exalting perspective – since
> it releases boldness of thought, stimulates the will to power,
> and substitutes for hope the idea of progress. An oppressive
> perspective, too, since man delivered over to himself has
> no recourse to other than himself, and the individual both
> exalts and abolishes himself at one and the same time.[5]

One of the most haunting of Piranesi's plates depicts the Campus
Martius as a deserted plain, around one side of which an equally
desolate River Tiber winds.

Plate 19: Piranesi: Il Campo Marzo dell'antica Roma, *Plate 2,
Scenographia, Campo Martii*

In the middle distance are vestigial depictions, tiny in scale, of some of the paramount structures of Roman times; the Pantheon, the theatre of Pompey, Domitian's Circus Agonalis (Piazza Navona). Surrounded by waste land, these stand like the remnants of some vanished tribe of nomads which has 'moved on'. In the foreground, by contrast, Piranesi piles up in a fantastic clutter fragments associated with the buildings of the Campus Martius. Survivors from the wreckage of time, they are listed and annotated with the dry avidity of the archaeological connoisseur. "These fragments have I shored against my ruins." Loss and desolation are graven upon this extraordinary plate, so disorientating for the viewer anxious to situate himself in time. The dense proliferation of eclectic ornament that we find in later volumes of Piranesi, such as the *Parere su l'Architettura* and the *Diverse Maniere d'Adornare I Cammini*, are also symptoms of a state of mind that is insatiable yet self-enclosed: tropically powerful exuberance amid ultimate futility. Decanted into the sensibility of this extraordinary man was all the looming desolation of modern times haunted by the waste of the temporal process, along with a Promethean – or Faustian – determination to fill the void with mammoth structures of technological domination. In Piranesi's case this was encapsulated in an image of Rome, which had been the fulcrum throughout many centuries of time redeemed within the orbit of eternity, an ideal symbolised in the great colonnade which stretches out its embracing arms to either side of St Peter's. Bernini's original conception for the Piazza had been that of an amphitheatre, and something of this still remains: "The oval piazza is not only the globe; it is also the whole universe revolving around the sun, symbolised by the obelisk . . . Overhead, there reigns, invisibly but magnificently, the heavenly theatre of the Church Triumphant, materially in the circle of saintly statues above the balustrade. The Piazza Obliqua is thus most completely the theatre: the amphitheatre of the Christian universe".[6]

That very same Piazza of St Peter's is depicted in one of the most famous of Piranesi's early *Vedute.*

Plate 20: Piranesi: Vedute di Roma, *Piazza di San Pietro*

The basilica is shown at a considerable distance, its facade starkly bisected by a black pin-like obelisk, the arms of the colonnade extending outward in curiously blank mechanical fashion. In the left foreground, however, are two coaches, in the larger of which, most elaborately gilded and bedizened, we discern through a window three upright, assured little figures of bewigged grand tourists. The florid vivacity of this foreground scene absorbs all the space beyond.

Plate 21: Piranesi: Vedute di Roma, *Piazza di San Pietro (detail)*

Here surely is an emblem of what the Holy City by the 18th century had become: no longer primarily a *caput mundi* for pilgrim souls and the devout, but the magnet of an appraising intelligentsia: tasting, tabulating, excavating; and, in part fired by Piranesi himself, imbibing inspiration for megalopolitan vistas of the future. Rome's gigantism becomes the visionary arena for the inspired ambition and the tragic nullity of the modern age, "the endless confrontation of man's will-power and infinity, the permanent injunction to go beyond present knowledge and achievement, the long evolution in which our own destinies are being enacted".[7]

For the late twentieth century legatees of the great break with traditional patterns initiated by the Enlightenment, their awareness of time colossally stretched by subsequent advances in geology, palaeontology and archaeology, the visionary ruins of Piranesi may well have a power of suggestion that goes beyond the conscious intention of their creator. Like other great works of art, they gather to themselves new meaning through the experience of later generations. The most prominent theorising by Piranesi himself about matters bearing on the temporal process is to be found in his attempt to establish the primacy of Etruscan influence on Roman architecture and decoration, resentful as he was at the new pre-eminence given to Greece as against Rome by the cognoscenti of the middle of the eighteenth century.[8] Taken in isolation, Piranesi's Etruscan obsession is merely a limited facet of the cultural history of the period. Yet it implies more, and evinces that wider concern with primitive origins prevalent in the eighteenth century, reflecting on the part of its intellectuals a fascination with time and the historical process. The prime name that comes to mind, in the Italian context, is that of Giambattista Vico. Certain shared attitudes to ancient Rome have stimulated recent Italian scholarship to posit a direct link between Piranesi and Vico, but attractive though the idea is, the evidence remains obstinately circumstantial.[9] Vico's *Scienza Nuova* (1744) stresses the creative imagination of primitive humanity peopling the sky with its gods, and the account he gives of savage giants and the like before the arrival of man as we know him would lead one to expect a suitably lengthened time-scheme in which to situate those alarming *bestioni*. Vico, however, like many early eighteenth century thinkers about the temporal origins of humanity, was hamstrung by his acceptance of a limited time-span conforming to the book of Genesis. Furthermore, Vico made a sharp separation between the history of the Hebrews and that of Gentiles, the former being exempt from the vicissitudes of successive stages and *ricorsi*. An aura of what the geologists call "deep time" is implicit in Vico, but his speculations were constrained by the Catholic orthodoxy of his time and place, to which he sincerely conformed. No such inhibition affected certain other eighteenth century thinkers contemplating the temporal status of mankind upon earth. Buffon, the prodigious naturalist of the 18th century Enlightenment, produced a time-scheme vastly exceeding the six thousand or so years derived from Biblical chronology, and in his *Histoire Naturelle*, which began to come out in 1749, he proposed a system of geological epochs spanning between one and two hundred thousand years. (This was for public consumption; his private opinion was more in the nature of ten million years.) Such speculations were rife in Enlightenment circles by the middle of the eighteenth century, but they had to wait upon empirical confirmation from such pioneers of geological science as James Hutton and, above all, Charles Lyell. In 1785 Hutton, the first to offer a purely empirical, uniformitarian account of geological change over very long periods of time, exclaimed at the conclusion of his *Theory of the Earth*: "We find no vestige of a beginning – no prospect of an end". The eighteenth century was

163

an age whose guiding ideal was the untrammeled pursuit of knowledge in all spheres, including those sciences concerned with the past. Something of its dedicated temper emerges from the opening passage of Buffon's *Des Epoques de la Nature*:

> *As in civil history documents are consulted, medals studied,*
> *ancient inscriptions deciphered, to determine the epochs of*
> *human revolutions and establish the dates of moral events,*
> *so in natural history it is necessary to rummage through the*
> *archives of the world, to draw from the bowels of the earth*
> *old monuments, collect their debris, and assemble in a*
> *body of proofs all indications of the physical changes which*
> *can carry us back to the different ages of nature. It is the*
> *only means of fixing points in the immensity of space and*
> *of placing a few milestones on the eternal path of time.*[10]

In that passage history shades into archaeology, which in the 18th century was ceasing to be mere antiquarianism, and increasingly becoming synthesised with the written documents of the historian.[11]

Piranesi, whose archaeological predilections are well known, had also, when young, been trained in Venice as an architect, and gained early acquaintance with the technical problems of hydraulics, engineering and various building methods. He brought to the observation of Roman ruins not just the visionary gaze of creative phantasy, and the exploratory fervour of the archaeologist, but the admiring appraisal of an architect fascinated by the technological feats of that most practical of imperial peoples. When we look at some of the technical plates that accompany his depiction of Roman remains, we do well to remember that Piranesi, though *persona grata* in Papal circles, had also had links with the advanced group around Lodoli in Venice, where a neo-classical ideal of functional utility in architecture was advocated; and when in Rome he moved among sophisticated groups with wide cosmopolitan ramifications. Such factors drew him into the orbit of the Enlightenment, whose principal organ of opinion-making, the French *Encyclopédie* – hostile to the traditional primacy of contemplation over action, and zealous for the secular advancement of humanity – attached much importance to up-grading the status of the mechanical as opposed to the liberal arts. Piranesi's plates depicting Roman tools and mechanisms bring home the practical inspiration to be drawn from the strenuous and exacting procedures of artisan and engineer. Yet those coldly technical plates are rampant with a mysteriously threatening energy. Piranesi transmogrifies, he does not merely depict: as in the plate depicting stone-laying techniques on the Appian Way; or in that illustrating the method of raising travertine blocks for building the tomb of Cecilia Metella, where the instruments illustrated are portentous with an obscurely surgical menace. The clinical energy of draftsmanship in such plates displays a fascinated responsiveness to the exercise of power: the constructive power of man the maker, man the fabricator. It is an Enlightenment disposition, nourishing itself, in Piranesi's case, upon the Roman achievement. Equally suggestive of the Enlightenment are certain of the figures who, amid Piranesi's cavernous vaults, stand in attitudes of elegant appraisal confronting the exhumed relics of the past, peering avidly at the contents of urn, sarcophagus, or other receptacle.

Plate 22: Piranesi: Le Antichità Romane *(1756), Volume III, Plate 7,*
Veduta dell'antica Via Appia

Mode, col quale furono alzati i groſſi Travertini, e gli altri Marmi nel fabbricare il gran Sepolcro di Cecilia Metella, oggi detto Capo di Bove.

Plate 23: Piranesi: Le Antichità Romane *(1756), Volume III, Plate 53, Method of rainsing Travertine blocks for Tomb of Cecilia Metella*

In such scenes the monumental ruins of the past, for all their overweening dimensions, become the arena for triumphant discoveries by the cognoscenti of modern and enlightened times, whom Justi amusingly compared to "aroused art-historians".[12] Such frenzy of discovery is to be seen in a plate from the *Antichità Romane*. In the left foreground three figures exhume from a sarcophagus an urn filled with the bones of freed servants and slaves: the Hamlet-like figure to the right of the group strikes an attitude of conventional melancholy; a middle figure rummages intently among the *disjecta membra* as they rattle forth from the urn; whilst the elegantly clad figure on the left stares upward with the rapt gaze and visionary fervour so characteristic of the 'Enlightened' enthusiast of reason.

Plate 24: Piranesi: Le Antichità Romane *(1756), Volume III, Plate 22, Ruins of the Burial Vault of Freed Slaves and Servants (detail)*

In another plate, this time depicting a cavernous underground site whose shadows are diversified by diagonal shafts of light – a subject that always seemed to stimulate Piranesi's imagination – confident elegant figures supervise the ant-like energies of others, who scramble up ladders or dilapidated stairways.

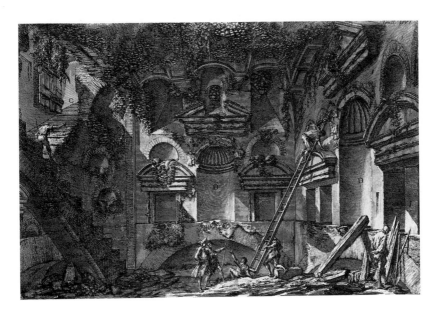

Plate 25: Piranesi: Le Antichità Romane *(1756), Volume III, Plate 56, Interior of Burial Vault*

To be noted, however, in the last plate is the characteristically small scale of Piranesi's animated human figures, something that is carried to an even further extreme in other plates. Such disproportion of scale between the human figure and its setting was of course a conventional device of the view-painters, or *vedutisti*, who ever since the mid-seventeenth century had exploited the pleasing aesthetic melancholy to be derived from Roman ruins, emphasising their grandeur by the strategic placement of some minute musing dilettante, or some tiny group of spectacularly ragged beggars. The sombre energy of Piranesi's imagination raised such devices to the level of tragic symbolism. As Mario Praz put it, the taste for ruins which, prior to Piranesi, had been more in the nature of a decorative phantasy, an arabesque, "put out teeth and claws; and, from having been a pleasing titillation of the skin, attacked the innards".[13]

Late seventeenth and eighteenth century speculations about the duration of the earth and the date of mankind's appearance thereon; the determination to uncover primitive origins; the pursuit of factual objectivity in historical and archaeological investigation; the un-earthing of Pompeii and Herculaneum; and, by no means least, the shock delivered by the Lisbon earthquake of 1756 to traditional notions concerning the purposeful harmony of divine creation: all were factors which "put teeth and claws" not just into the cult of ruins, but into the whole European response to the time-process. Along with the Enlightenment exhilaration of discovery there went, concurrently, a more poignant awareness of the traditional trope of time's destructiveness: its immensity of span and its cosmic futility. Such were to be the shadows attendant on the new deity of Progress. Something of this complex and ambiguous process, only sporadically underway in Piranesi's time, but fundamental for understanding the disposition of a good part of modern humanity, was captured by Piranesi not in any theoretical formulation but by the prescient gaze of imaginative intuition. The vast corroded bulks and dizzy diminishing perspectives where Piranesian midgets peer and prod and ponder, the awesome chiaroscuro incised by his tools and his acids with such delicately graded virtuosity, reflect some of the disturbing implications in the thought of the period. Burke, in his speculations on the sublime, wrote of the terror of things multiplied seemingly without end.[14]

Piranesi gave visual expression to that terror. In a print of the Appian Way, the Chaplinesque figure in the middle distance is diminished and isolated by the monumentally delineated flagstones of the road, as it stretches massively to infinity. Yet the

Plate 26:

Piranesi: Antichità d'Albano e di Castel Gandolfo, *Plate 25, Pavement and sides of the Appian Way*

171

abrupt way in which the plate is cut off at the top seems also to hem in the space, thus creating that double mood, of constriction as well as endlessness, so characteristic of much of Piranesi's work. In another print, depicting the buttressed foundations of the Mausoleum of Hadrian, still extant in Rome as the Castel San Angelo, the tiny human figures at the top outer edge are barely visible, whilst the colossal bulk of serried stone presses forward and downward to crush the eye of the viewer and dwarf the picture-frame. We barely take in the presence of other tiny figures

Plate 27: Piranesi: Le Antichità Romane *(1756),
Volume IV, Plate 9, Foundations of
the Mausoleum of Hadrian*

172

on the bottom platform, standing in the familiar poses of elegant appraisal: "Regardless of their doom, the little victims play". Meanwhile, some primal cataclysm of stone seems immanent in the brooding mountainous mass. In yet other prints of Piranesi, etiolated midgets are barely visible amid the dense shadows of crumbling monuments, where parasitic creepers entwine around cracked column and mutilated marble, and shrubs or trees push through the crumbling corners and mouldering recesses of vaulted burial-chambers. In such prints, Focillon remarked, in his still unsurpassed monograph, "the monuments are like geological remains".[15] Giant wrecks of man-made grandeur and the intertwining overgrowth of natural forces unite in conveying the evanescence of mankind amidst the devastations of time. Nature and monument loom as one colossal minatory presence proclaiming: *Memento Mori*. There is not only a great sense of loss in Piranesi, the sense of time's depredations. There is also 'lostness', a sense of being lost: overwhelmed, obliterated, stranded. In his print of the Baths of Trajan the eye moves dejectedly from one heap of ruins to another, resting nowhere. It fastens momentarily on one or other of the minute human figures, but soon swivels away and around. They give no help. They seem merely to underline the sense of straying aimlessly amidst a heap of *objets trouvés*: those humps of burgeoning vegetation and crumbling stone which symbolise the constant metamorphosis of the temporal process. "Time falls through all the world of Piranesi, thick and palpable", R.M. Adams has remarked, "even his prisons are like vast dark sundials through which isolated and interrupted shafts of day strike to mark off the leaden hours".[16]

Plate 28: Piranesi: Le Vedute di Roma, *The Baths of Trajan (formerly known as Baths of Titus)*

Loss and disorientation in time, as found in some of the more expressive of Piranesi's Roman ruin etchings, are paralleled in his most famous set of etchings, *I Carceri* (The Prisons) by disorientation in space. Confronted with these strange works (e.g. prints VII and XIV) the eye swings distractedly from one plane to another, in a constant agitation of pseudo-directedness. Diagonal stairways commence, skew away at an unexpected angle, only to be blocked abruptly by one of the great sombre piers that support the vaulting; vaulting which in its turn encloses nothing coherent, just a receding succession of endless vestibules and foyers. Tenuous cat-walks are slung from nowhere, coil around the piers, disappear into a void. Tiny spectral figures randomly populate

Plate 29: Piranesi: Carceri d'Invenzione, *(Second State) Plate VII*

Plate 30: Piranesi: Carceri d'Invenzione, *(Second State) Plate XIV*

some of the stairways and cat-walks, gaze down into the depths below, or engage in some mute colloquy. Chains loop nonchalantly between stanchions. A strange torpedo-like object with great grim spikes hints of formidable torments always at the ready. Huge coils of rope swing down and across the picture-frame, their swooping arcs assertively at odds with the curving vaults, the labyrinthine stairways, the spidery catwalks, and the solid piers that swell goitrously into watchtowers. A Baroque addiction to the diagonal, which in Piranesi was fostered by his early acquaintance with the stage-designs of the Bibbiena family, recoils upon itself and devours its own substance. The unceasing deployment of contradictory diagonals, the wrenched perspectives, give the eye no rest.[17] The frenzy of self-cancelling angles of vision recedes into infinity:

> The stretching of space testifies to an immeasurable transcendence by space of any properly human world. It has the effect of making the viewer immediately aware of the absolute transcendence of space in relation to man. With Piranesi there appears an inverted space, a space that accentuates distance and, in the very act of widening, shrinks; and by the same token makes the human figure appear more vulnerable, since it finds itself thrown there, as if lost.[18]

The perverse paradoxes of the visual space in *I Carceri* rivet the eye of the beholder upon a totally asymmetrical world. The ideal of harmony which, in various guises, had been the cosmological and cultural ideal of Europe down to the seventeenth century, is imploded. "Piranesi annuls any nostalgia for the age-old cult of unity".[19] A unity whose most potent visual symbol had been that of the circle, even if only – as was the case with Nicholas of Cusa – a circle whose "centre was everywhere and circumference nowhere". The cosmological image of the circle, with its origins in Pythagoreanism and neo-Platonism, was, as we have seen, endemic to the neo-Platonised Christianity that came to fruition in the Renaissance and Baroque period, the climactic visual icon of that ancient ideal being, somewhat ambiguously, the Rome of Bernini and the Baroque Popes. Galileo himself, so undermining a figure for much that the Baroque Popes stood for, still retained a traditional neo-Platonic awe of the circle as the perfect cosmological figure, and "this had caused him to endorse the belief, common to Platonism and Aristotelianism, in the perfection – the privileged status – of the circle not only from a mathematical or aesthetic but also from a mechanical point of view".[20] The notion of a spherical, essentially finite cosmos did not long survive other aspects of Galileo's activities. Nevertheless, even when, by mid-seventeenth century, the implications of Galileo's and Fr Scheiner's telescopic reports on the expanding heavens had been infiltrated willy-nilly by the heterodox spatial theories of Giordano Bruno, the effect upon the religious imagination was far from being wholly negative. God was to persist in a more or less harmonious relation with the new spatiality for another century or so. Not surprisingly, some of the writings of Kircher offered evidence of this: his *Itinerarium Ecstaticum* of 1656, though settling for the compromise cosmology of Tycho Brahe, in which the earth remained stable but the other planets circle around the sun, showed eloquent enthusiasm for the new-found spatial immensities, taken as manifesting, on a hitherto unimaginable scale, the divine power.

The later seventeenth and early eighteenth centuries were to be the great age of physico-theologians, as well as of poets similarly disposed, for whom God was the harmoniser and guarantor of the Newtonian systems of mechanical law: acceptance of the new cosmology did not preclude constant tributes to the spatial virtuosity of the deity, enthusiastic if not mystical. The poet James Thomson exclaims in *The Seasons*, "Inspiring God! who, boundless Spirit all,/ And unremitting Energy, pervades,/ Adjusts, sustains, and agitates the whole". Potentially unsettling for such attitudes, however, had been Henry More's *Enchiridion Metaphysicum* of 1671, which virtually divinised space itself and attributed to the deity incorporeal extension as a prime attribute.[21] More had some influence upon Newton, who hazarded at one place in his *Opticks* that space was the "sensorium of deity"[22] This type of speculation gave unintended sanction to a spatialisation of the divine, which thereupon fused with a Nature already in part divinised by the attribute of Sublimity. For heterodox thought of the eighteenth century such fusion was to prove an attractive means of preserving, on altered terms, the ancient ideal of cosmic unity. The whole story has been brilliantly told in Hélène Tuzet's *Le Cosmos et l'Imagination.*[23] The immanentist pantheism of romantic poets and theoreticians, variously conjuring the interpenetration of mind and matter within some intuited holistic unity and, like German Absolute Idealism of the same period, bearing the marks of an ultimate origin in neo-Platonic and hermetic sources,[24] was to be the last comprehensive attempt of the European religious imagination to sustain the ancient ideal of cosmological harmony. In the course of the eighteenth century, however, the grounds for such harmonious integration were being inexorably subverted, not only by the sustained demolitions of a Hume or a Kant, but also by the incessant snipings of the more radical of the French *philosophes*, of which this instance from Diderot may be taken as typical:

> How many maimed, failed worlds have been dissolved, and are now perhaps dissolving at every moment, in those distant spaces where motion combines and will continue to combine accumulations of matter until they have attained some form in which to persevere. What is this world but a

179

composite, subject to changes which all indicate a
continuous tendency to destruction; a rapid succession of
beings which follow one another, flourish, and disappear; a
fleeting symmetry; a momentary order.[25]

Two twentieth century comments on Piranesi read like glosses on the existential implications of the Diderot passage. Manfredo Tafuri writes that Piranesi "presents organisms that pretend to have a centrality but that never achieve one."[26] To which let us add the following comment by Marguerite Yourcenar: "This world of Piranesi, deprived of a centre is also in perpetual expansion . . . This world closed in upon itself is mathematically infinite".[27] Yourcenar's hint – "a world in perpetual expansion" – needs to be developed, since it points us to the element of power-worship in Piranesi's phantasies, his Promethean *volontarisme*, which is as important to grasp as his proto-Romantic melancholy.

Let us remember that Piranesi's intention in his Roman etchings, including even *I Carceri*, was far more positive than Romantic despair or modern Angst would have it. Piranesi admired the constructive genius of the Romans, and hoped that his etchings, one set of which is called *Le Magnificenze di Roma*, would with all their technical as well as picturesque properties inspire a comparable constructive effort of will among modern architects; Piranesi, beside sharing Vico's conclusions on the autonomy of Roman civilisation as ultimately derived from Etruscan sources, also echoed Vico's belief in *"il ricorso delle cose umane nel risorgere che fanno le nazioni"*[28] (the undying capacity of great nations [such as Rome] for cultural revival). It has further been suggested, by Calvesi, that in *I Carceri* Piranesi was paying hyperbolic tribute not just to the constructive genius of Rome but also to its achievements in civil order, law – and punishment. If we take to heart two inscriptions in etching number XVI of *I Carceri*, this carries conviction. One inscription above a relief depicting prisoners on the column to the right – *infame sceluss . . . ri infelici suspe . . .* – is a paraphrase of a passage of Livy's history of Rome (Book I, 26) describing an instance of justifiable punishment; another inscription, on a nearby Egyptian lotus column – *ad terrorem increscem audaciae* – is also taken from Book I of Livy (33), and alludes to the creation of the dreaded Mamertine Prison on the Capitoline hill. Such memorialising of Roman punitive prowess in the concluding etching of the whole *I Carceri* series – it was one of three added to the set by Piranesi for his heavily re-worked second state edition – could lend plausibility to Calvesi's further suggestion that *I Carceri* show structural features which make them an imaginative enlargement of the Roman Mamertine prison.[29] The etchings are a harshly constructive celebration, not a paranoid phantasy; and it is easy to agree with Lorenz Eitner that an important source of their sublimity is the exaltation of human energy, made manifest in architecture.[30]

Piranesi called on his death-bed for a copy of Livy: "I have no faith but this", he proclaimed, "Repose is unworthy of a citizen of Rome; let me look again at my models, my designs, my engravings".[31] To which let us juxtapose the remark of Piranesi quoted at the beginning of this chapter: "I need to produce great ideas, and I believe that were I given the planning of a new universe, I would be mad enough to undertake it". A final, crystallising turn can now be given to our understanding of the artist.

181

Piranesi confronts us as an instance of that will to power implicit in the Enlightenment admiration for the austere civic virtues of antiquity, which found visual expression in the neo-classic style of the late eighteenth century. Although much of Piranesi's later work in the *Parere su l'Architettura* and in *Diverse Maniere d'Adornare I Cammini* shows symptoms of an eclectic *horror vacui* which fits no formula of the period, but portends the historicist clutter of the nineteenth century, his unconsciously sinister and grandiose tributes to Roman monumentality were to inspire the grimly utopian neo-classic phantasies of a Boullée and a Ledoux.[32] Despite the vegetal deliquescence that clings around all Piranesi's Roman ruins, they loom as stupendous tributes to the Roman will to endure through time: a neo-classic *exemplum virtutis*. Mario Praz, writing of late eighteenth century neo-classicism, has a sentence that applies to Piranesi: "It is the ancient world seen through the eyes of Plutarch – a school of will-power, of energy, of heroic duty, an ideal and idolised region in which classicism becomes, romantically, the material of dreams".[33] Dreams not just of the past, romantic in decay, but of the future, too; of mankind's subduing the earth through technology amid vistas of architectural gigantism, whose potential for horror is caught by the numbing iteration of Piranesi's *I Carceri*: emblems of power in the pure state, where humanity triumphs in the will but dies in the spirit, as testified by those stricken homunculi who populate the galleries and stairways of the plates.[34]

"Un sovrumana potenza regnante su un caos," (sovereign power presiding over chaos), was the way Focillon crystallised his over-riding impression of Piranesi's work. The Enlightenment dream, bequeathed to modern times, of a rational utopia

constructed for the civic self-glorification of humanity, stands revealed through Piranesi's genius in all its sombre self-immolating aspiration. Always at its back are the appalling stretches of "time before and time after": the abyss of transience and non-being that lurks amid the shaggy desolation of his most powerful plates. This is a world of pure will, trapped amid its own desolate sublimity; yet a portent too of the transformative powers that in the 19th century were to inject sheer transience with the dynamics of Progress. In the words of Starobinski:

> *What was developing in the late 18th century was a Promethean* volontarisme, *intent on dominating nature and controlling history. Man's will-power created a new spatio-temporal universe in which to develop and assume material form. The co-ordinates in which the mind had henceforth to act were Nature and Time. By comparison, we could affirm that the volontarism of the Renaissance and the Baroque period was nothing more than a search for the illustrious stability of rational man, upon a background of extra-temporal, eternal values.*[35]

Notes to Chapter V

1. J.G. Legrand, 'Notice sur la Vie et les ouvrages de G.-B. Piranesi', reprinted in *Nouvelles de l'Estampe*, no. 5, 1969, 222

2. Karl Lehmann, 'Piranesi as Interpreter of Roman Architecture', Smith College Museum of Art (Northampton, Mass., 1961) 93-4

3. E. Kaufmann, *Architecture in the Age of Reason* (Dover Books, 1967) 106

4. Manfredo Tafuri, *The Sphere and the Labyrinth* (M.I.T. Press, 1987) 35

5. J. Fabre, *Lumières et Romantisme* (C. Klincksieck, Paris, 1963) vi

6. T. Kitao, *The Circle and the Oval in the Square of St Peter's* (New York, 1974) 26

7. J. Starobinski, *The Invention of Liberty* (Skira, 1964) 209

8. cf. *Della Magnificenza ed Architettura de'Romani* (1761) and *Diverse Maniere d'Adornare I Cammini* (1769) in *G.B. Piranesi: The Polemical Works*, ed. J. Wilton-Ely, (Gregg International Publishers Ltd., 1972)

9. Maurizio Calvesi, in his Introduction to the Italian translation of H Focillon's G.B. Piranesi (Bologna, 1967). See also Calvesi's later article, 'Ideologia e Riferimenti delle "Carceri"', in *Piranesi tra Venezia e l'Europa*, a cura di E Bettagno, (Firenze, 1983)

10. *Oeuvres Complètes* de Buffon, I (Paris, 1857), 479

11. cf. A. Momigliano, 'Ancient History and the Antiquarian', *Journal of the Warburg and Courtauld Institute*, 13-14, (1950-1)

12. *Winckelmann und Seine Zeitgenossen*, Band 2, (Phaidon Verlag, Köln, 1956), 436: "Sind es jene Elenden, die der Orient in die Einöden ausstiess; oder die Unsauberen, die der Prophet in Babels Trümmern schaute, oder sind es aufgeregte Kunsthistoriker?"

13. G.B. Piranesi, *I Carceri*: Introduzione di Mario Praz, (Rizzoli, 1975), 11

14. *A Philosophical Inquiry into the Origin of our Ideas of the Sublime and the Beautiful*, Part II, Sections 7, 8 and 9

15. H. Focillon, *G.-B. Piranesi, 1720-1778*, (Paris 1918), published in Italian as *Giovanni Battista Piranesi*, ed. M. Calvesi and A. Monferini (Bologna, 1967) 215

16. *The Roman Stamp* (University of California Press, 1974) 184

17. John Wilton-Ely, whose writings are a steady corrective to the

romantic phantasising and modern Angst which can be too easily read into *I Carceri* series, goes so far as to remark: "As never before, the Western system of pictorial space is questioned with all its implications concerning the nature of perception. The challenge was not to be met again until the revolution of Cubism". *The Mind and Art of G.-B. Piranesi*, (Thames and Hudson, London, 1978) 85

18. Georges Poulet, 'Piranèse et les Poètes Romantiques Français', *La Nouvelle Revue Française*', Vol. 13 (160) 1966, 665

19. Manfredo Tafuri, 'Borromini e Piranesi: La Città come "Ordine Infranto"'; in *Piranesi tra Venezia e l'Europa*, a cura di A Bettagno (Firenze 1983) 101

20. E. Panofsky, *Galileo as Critic of the Arts*, (Nijhoff, The Hague, 1954).

21. cf. Edward Grant, *Much Ado About Nothing, Theories of Space and Vacuum from the Middle Ages to the Scientific Revolution* (C.U.P., 1981) 221- 228

22. Grant, op. cit., 246-7. cf. also E.A. Burtt, *The Metaphysical Foundations of Modern Physical Science* (R.K.P., 1924), 258

23. *Le Cosmos et l'Imagination* (J. Corti, Paris, 1963)

24. J. Viatte, *Les Sources Occultes du Romantisme* (Paris, 1928)

25. D. Diderot, *Lettre sur les Aveugles* (Textes Littéraires Français, Droz, 1951), 43-4

26. Op. cit., Tafuri, 27

27. 'Les Prisons Imaginaires de Piranèse', *Nouvelle Revue Française* Vol. 9 (67) 1961, 2

28. Wilton-Ely, op. cit., p.67 (cf. also Robert Adam, who saw a good deal of Piranesi whilst in Rome: "So amazing and ingenious fancies as he has produced in the different plans of the Temples, Baths and Palaces and other buildings I never saw, and are the greatest fund for inspiring and instilling invention in any lover of architecture that can be imagined". Quoted in John Fleming's *Robert Adam and his*

Circle in Edinburgh and London, (London, 1962)

29. Calvesi, 'Ideologia e Riferimento delle "Carceri"', in *Piranesi tra Venezia e l'Europa*, op. cit., 352ff

30. Lorenz Eitner, 'Cages, Prisons and Captives in 18th Century Art', in *Images of Romanticism* (Yale University Press, 1978), 26

31. Quoted in Mario Praz, *On Neo-Classicism*, 'Revolutionary Classicism' (Thames & Hudson, 1969), 195

32. cf. Wilton-Ely, op. cit., 120-1

33. *On Neo-Classicism*, 197

34. " . . . Câbles, machines, roues et catapultes, en raison de leurs dimensions multipilées, deviennent des engins d'une puissance effrayante, puissance qui semble menacer l'homme de destruction . . ." Poulet, op. cit., 665

35. J. Starobinski, op. cit., 207

CHAPTER VI

TIME AS PROGRESS:

THE RISORGIMENTO

Starobinski's words bear aptly on the most comprehensive portent at the beginning of the 19th century of Promethean energy uncircumscribed by traditional notions of the sacred and the eternal: Napoleon, and the centralizing bureaucracy of the Napoleonic state-apparatus.

Admittedly, there were certain appearances to the contrary: Napoleon crowned himself emperor in 1804 in the presence of Pope Pius VII – a humiliation for the pope whom he was later actually to exile from Rome; he nominated his son King of Rome, thereby staking a claim to the ancient Holy Roman Empire deriving from Charlemagne. The cradle of the infant King was designed by Prudhon with all the oppressive solidity characterising First Empire style, and encrusted with traditional imperial symbolism – a laurel-wreath of glory, an eagle, the goddess Fame, an emblem of the River Tiber.[1] Napoleon thus envisaged Rome as a second city, after Paris, of a revived Charlemagnesque Empire, but one where the scales would be decisively tipped in favour of *regnum* rather than *sacerdotium*. Yet he himself, his armies, and his state-bureaucracy were the most decisive of breaks ever experienced by the old European world-order.

The French wars of Napoleon, originally initiated by the revolutionary armies of the Directory, released energies that led to the eventual emergence of a plurality of nation-states which cast off dynastic and ecclesiastical tutelage. Each, under liberal auspices, was to claim freedom and autonomy for the individual, as well as for the nation as linguistic-territorial entity; yet, by virtue of the power-vacuum created, each fostered, in the short or long term, a centralising bureaucratic state-apparatus. Such state-apparatus, in the ideal logic envisaged by Hegel, its omniscient encomiast, excludes any higher, independent realm of spiritual values. The sovereign state subordinates religion to itself, either tyrannically, or in the emasculating guise of toleration, thus fostering a pervasive secularism that sidelines the transcendental and the sacred. Such has been the fundamental, covert logic of Progress in modern times, in a variety of forms, some benign, some far from such. This, fundamentally, was what lay behind the notorious formulation of Pius IX in the *Syllabus Errorum* of 1864: "If anyone thinks that the Roman Pontiff can and should reconcile himself and come to terms with progress, with liberalism and with modern civilisation, let him be anathema".

Thus did Pius IX reformulate the primacy of the spiritual realm in opposition to the centralising State, which Eternal Rome of the papacy had claimed to embody, with varying degrees of emphasis, since the late 11th century onwards. This bore some relation to an analogous perception of de Tocqueville, the aristocratic liberal who was such a stern yet urbane critic of democratic trends in the 19th century. In 1855, in his book on The Old Régime and the Revolution, he observes that not popular sovereignty, but centralisation, had been the achievement of revolutionary France and its ensuing Napoleonic régime, the whole endeavour of a modern state within its own dominions being "to draw to itself and absorb in its unity all the fragments of authority and influence which were formerly dispersed among a crowd of secondary powers, orders, classes, professions, families, and individuals, scattered as it were throughout the social organism. The world had never seen a power like it since the fall of the Roman Empire"[2].

It was thus only to be expected that, in 1808, the papacy – in the shape of Pius VII, symbol of opposition to the engulfing Prometheanism of modern statehood – should be exiled, and a Napoleonic regime imposed on Rome. The papal states, like the city itself, were subjected to secular control, and a more efficient and centralised administration – admittedly much needed – was instituted. Rome, in the days of Napoleon's glory, seemed destined to become the adjunct of a new secularising *imperium* cast in the mould, both sinister and beneficent, of modern progress. Rome's centuries-old claim to be the second, papal and sacrosanct consummation of the Roman Empire, was comprehensively truncated.

After the defeat of Napoleon and the temporary restoration of the old dynastic régimes by the Congress of Vienna, Rome and the papacy appeared for a spell to regain more even than they had lost in the closing pre-Revolutionary years of the 18th century: Jesuits re-instated, advantageous concordats negotiated, temporal powers restored in the papal states. Those states, however, like the rest of Italy from the 1820s through to 1848 and beyond, were subject to recurrent subversion by the now irrepressible liberal-nationalist zeal unleashed by the French revolutionary and Napoleonic disruption of the old European order: the Carbonari, a revolutionary grouping adorned by Byron's support, were typical. The greatest scourge of restored papal and dynastic hegemony, however, called itself Young Italy; its leader, Mazzini, an archetypal nationalist and populist, was religious in the heterodox pantheistic vein of so many Romantics. He envisaged an expanding future of free peoples issuing in some international communion when humanity would be harmonised with the cosmos through the immanent dynamic of progress. The *anomie* that lay in wait for totally free and isolated individuals, a potential threat in Enlightenment ideals of pure Reason – so presciently symbolised by Piranesi's *I Carceri* – would be overcome by making of history, in J.L. Talmon's words, "an ally instead of an enemy, something to be fulfilled rather than overcome. The progress of time was conceived as steady advance towards higher integration". Time is no longer the Christian neo-Platonic reflection of the Eternal. Time is no longer the destroyer, the flail of transience. Time is the conduit of destiny eliciting from its innards, like Demogorgon in Shelley's *Prometheus Unbound,* that potential for future progress in goodness which had been perverted by static ideals of Eternity – of which Rome had hitherto been prime symbol – and undermined by doctrines of sin and the necessity of divine redemption. "All politically Messianic trends", continues Talmon, "considered Christianity, at times religion as such, and always the historic form of Christianity, as the arch-enemy. Indeed they triumphantly proclaimed themselves substitutes for it. Their own message of salvation was utterly incompatible with the basic Christian doctrine, that of original sin, with its vision of history as the story of the fall, and its denial of man's power to attain salvation by his own exertions".[3] Inspired by such politically messianic trends, which pullulated in the rhetorical steam-bath of Romantic-liberal and nationalist rhetoric of the early 19th century, Mazzini was able to give fundamental impetus to the ideal of a Third Rome, the offspring not of Eternity, but of Time and Progress, thus superseding the First and Second Romes of the Empire and the Popes. Rome, at the head of Italy, was envisaged as consummating that ideal of united nationhood which, with varied ideological trappings, was to be the new religion of the 19th and 20th centuries; it would be the spiritual centre of an ever-expanding unity, enacting an humanitarian parody of that universalist mission of the Church which in earlier chapters we encountered in the Jesuit-Baroque Catholicism of the 16th and 17th centuries. This all lies open in the words of Mazzini himself, written when the forces of the Risorgimento had suffered temporary set-back after the expulsion of Garibaldi's troops from the short-lived Roman Republic of 1849, and the reinstallation of the papal regime of Pio Nono under the protection of Louis-Napoleon's French troops:

Just as, to the Rome of the Caesars, which through Action united a great part of Europe, there succeeded the Rome of

the Popes, which united Europe and America in the realm
of the spirit, so the Rome of the People will succeed them
both, to unite, in a faith that will make Thought and Action
one, Europe, America and every part of the terrestrial globe
. . . Write upon your hearts and on your banner: We
acknowledge one God in Heaven, and one interpreter of
His law upon earth, the People.[4]

Latent in that last phrase of Mazzini are portents of what the future
was to hold for much of Europe in the course of the 20th century:
Caesarism and populist totalitarianism as the so-called 'Will of the
People', high-jacked by demagogues and *condottieri* to the Left
and the Right.

Italy achieved its Risorgimento. Cavour, Prime Minister of
Piedmont in the service of the Savoy dynasty, exploited various
tensions among the great powers of mid-19th century Europe, in
particular the complicated ambitions of Napoleon III, whose ability
to defend the papacy's temporal power vanished in the wake of
his defeat in 1870 by Bismarckian Germany. Rome was to be the
capital of a new, progressive, modernised Italy, so that even a
contemporary traditionalist of independent views, Stefanucci Ala,
could say that "whilst the press, the telegraph, and steam-power
endow the collaborative spirit of the peoples with new and
marvellous wings, the spirit that animates the mass will always
have in Rome its sure foundation".[5] Faith in technology,
industrialism, science – scientific congresses were specially highly
esteemed – abounded among the liberal elements of the
Risorgimento, with their positivist and secularising tendencies. Less
visionary and apocalyptic than the Mazzinian strand of the

Risorgimento, they were anxious that Italy as well as Rome should, like the rest of Europe, become thoroughly *embourgeoisé* at last. Would the new Third Rome, with its varied and contradictory ideological strands, be worthy of its destiny to be an "army of soldiers, an industrial company, a scientific laboratory, and people of workers",[6] pondered Hippolyte Taine in 1865, in the concluding section of his book on Rome, where the celebrations of Holy Week convinced him that he had witnessed the veritable finale of old papal Rome and its pomp.

'Finale' would indeed appear to have been the apt word when, on 20 September 1870, the Pope was expelled from the Quirinal, after an assault through Rome's Porta Pia by Victor Emmanuel II's Piedmontese troops. Thereafter he and his successors would never emerge again from the Vatican City, final enclave of the temporal power of the papacy, until the Concordat with Mussolini in 1929. By that time, however, the nationalism that for Mazzini had been the visionary prefiguration of a harmonious international community had been tainted by two generations of intermittently shady parliamentary manoeuvring. It had also experienced the emergence of that Social Darwinism which is latent in all nationalism, however shrouded by liberal or even by socialist rhetoric: "Those socialists" Croce remarked, hinting at the zest for colonial expansion – Eritrean, Abyssinian, Tripolitanian – in which modern Italy was belatedly emulating the other European powers, "were no more, but no less patriotic than the rest of the Italian parties".[7]

Prominent among the exponents of this burgeoning nationalist imperialism of the new Third Rome was the superficially implausible figure of a 'decadent' poet and novelist famous over all Europe for his perverse and eloquent eroticism: Gabriele D'Annunzio. D'Annunzio was subject to an explosive brand of Nietzschean Will to Power as well, so much so that the hero of one of his novels, *Le Vergini delle Rocce*, wonders at length upon which of three exemplary virgins he shall father a son whom he envisages, Napoleonically, as being a worthy future King of Rome! D'Annunzio's resurgent Third-Rome imperialism was not always quite so bizarre, and in one of the Odes of his *Elettra*, he provides material that exemplifies Talmon's analysis of why Mussolinian Fascism, with its imperialist ambitions, made such a swift appeal to post-Risorgimento Italy. Admittedly the Risorgimento was in part republican, anti-clerical, left-liberal and bourgeois. In the early part of the 20th century, this Piedmontese, north Italian, Cavour-ish strand was continued by dextrous parliamentary operators like Giolitti, who presided over that unheroic *Italietta* so resented and despised by D'Annunzio and his inflamed companions. They saw it, in D'Annunzio's words, as "Italy . . . a *pension de famille*, a museum, a horizon painted with Prussian blue for international honeymooners.[8]" All along, however, there was the countervailing inspiration of the myth of Rome, the Third Rome, heir to the Universal Church, itself heir to the Roman Empire, that prepotent symbol of domination: so that Talmon can even remark that both "Left and Right were fascinated by defiance, force, action . . . The smugness and complacency of humanitarian ethics, petty utilitarianism, and the abhorrence of hazard, risk, adventure and cruelty were condemned or ridiculed as signs of decadence. Starting like Maurice Barrès, and narcissistic priests in the temple of the *culte du moi*, Oriani, Corradini and of course D'Annunzio shifted from disdain of the crowd and the hoi

194

polloi into a Promethean posture."[9]

D'Annunzio wrote his proto-fascist Ode *To Rome* in 1900, to commemorate the Piedmontese attack of 20 September 1870 on the Porta Pia. He linked this event to an Italic myth in Livy, where a carving of the Great Mother, brought across the sea to redeem Rome at a moment of national crisis, was greeted by a pure Virgin of the people:

> *Today, however, will not see that pure hand bearing an image venerated in foreign shrines, but the Power of Humanity, the sacred spirit engendered from the heart of the People in peace and war, the glory of the Earth created by the divine inspiration of the Will, and transfigured by innumerable works of light and shade, love and hatred, life and death – the beauty of human destiny, of mankind which seeks god in its own creation. For in you (Rome), an indestructible imprint, the Power of Mankind, will take form and pressure, instituted on the Capitol and in the Forum, and set over against mankind's Shame . . .* [10]

D'Annunzio's values were vitalist and neo-Nietzschean as well as Roman and Imperial, but despite the concluding reference to the 'Shame' to which clericalism had reduced the Church, D'Annunzio's Roman values were less alien to a bellicose and be-glamorised Catholicism than to that moderate bourgeois-liberalism which was a part of post-Risorgimento Italy. Let us dwell for a moment on the theatrical religiosity of the neo-Baroque Church of the 19th and early 20th century, as seen by Ugo Ogetti. An admiring friend of D'Annunzio, and a talented journalist of the

Right, Ogetti describes illuminations of St Peter's on an occasion in the 1920's:

> *The basilica has disappeared, now nothing can be seen of it but the lights. The cupola is exalted alone in the sky, encircled by six crowns of torches, with each column of the lantern transformed into a column of fire, and, over all, the Cross . . . The colossi of St Peter and St Paul on guard over the steps, the apostles on the attic of the basilica, the saints in a row on the colonnade, are now no more than bodiless phantasms, spurned into darkness by the blazing apparition of the cross over the mountain of light.*[11]

Such a scene reminds us, by vehement symbolism, that throughout the 19th century emergence of a 'Third Rome', and well into the 20th century, *Seconda Roma*, the Rome of the Popes, with its aims and ambitions, had continued to exist. In the 1830's and 1840's there had even been an abortive coalescence of the two. Here the figure of Vincenzo Gioberti calls for a word. Gioberti was a prominent priest-politician of the mid-19th century, even briefly prime minister of Piedmont in 1848-9, before the dominance of Cavour. Gioberti's great period of influence on the Roman church, however, had occurred earlier, in the years just before 1846, when Pius IX, a putative liberal, had assumed the triple tiara, as successor to a trio of grim intransigents, Leo XII, Pius VIII and Gregory XVI. This last had promulgated *Mirari Vos* in 1832, an encyclical 'hammer of the liberals' which gave a strong foretaste of what Pius IX himself was to proclaim in the 1864 *Syllabus Errorum*, which he added to his own *Quanta Cura* encyclical. By then Pius

196

IX *(Pio Nono)* had long ceased to figure in liberal circles as a version of the *Papa Angelico* of later medieval prophecy, for he had clearly discerned the religious indifferentism, human self-sufficiency and state-supremacism implicit in the liberal-nationalist movements of the age – "Struggling" – in Ranke's superb definition of the spirit of the 19th century – "among violent dissensions towards unknown goals, self-confident yet ever-unsatisfied".[12] By the *Syllabus Errorum*, by calling the First Vatican Council, and by promulgating the doctrine of papal infallibility, Pius IX put behind him not just the doctrines of Mazzini, but even the earlier compromise of Gioberti, to which he might have been interpreted as seeming sympathetic in the early 1840's. "I will not do what Mazzini wants", he had said, as well as adding, "and I cannot do what Gioberti wants."[13]

What had Gioberti wanted? Italian unity – the Risorgimento ideal – but in a federal system under the presidency of the Pope. Post-Rousseauist populism *à la* Mazzini, Italian nationalism, Christian providentialism, neo-papalism, and the old Baroque neo-Platonist ideal of harmony between the terrestrial and celestial realms, all simmered in one turbidly anachronistic brew:

> *The Catholic religion which had created the morality and civilisation of Italy, the people selected by the Almighty to smooth the path of the Gospel, just as the Israelites were miraculously chosen and formed for the same task; and just as the God-Man established in Jerusalem the first seeds of the Gospel, the chief of the apostles transplanted it to Rome . . . Italy will be the sacred nation in the great body of redemptive peoples, a society of men rescued from itself,*

under the universal law – one, free, flourishing and holy
and expressing the concord of heaven and earth . . .
Rome the eternal city not subject to the changes and power
of time, because it represents the immanent Idea
counterpoised to the transient: an Idea truly Platonic, Italian
in origin, because it goes back to Pythagoras, but re-made,
perfected, fertilised by a divine seed through the work of
Christianity; the Vicar of Christ, spiritual monarch of the
Church, as well as universal arbitrator and pacifier of the
Christian peoples, in particular those of Italy . . .[14]

Gioberti's neo-Guelf eclecticism had no future. The Risorgimento rejected it in favour of a secular nationalism tinged with progressive religiosity. Pius IX rejected it in favour of the universal rôle of a papacy now deemed infallible, thus balancing the loss of temporal power in 1870. And despite the aura of defeat that seemingly shrouded the Church in the 19th century, its compensating triumphs should not be overlooked: unprecedented missionary expansion across the globe, the founding of new orders of religious, the abundance of sanctity and the multiplying of canonisations and beatifications, the articulation under Leo XIII, Pius IX's successor, of doctrines mediating between capitalism and socialism, the tighter inter-locking of all parts of the universal Church to its one centre in Rome.[15] "For both sides – Risorgimento and papacy – Rome was the city of their dreams. For the one side the city was the home of their new aspiration, for the other side it was their eternal home on earth."[16] Well into the 20th century there were those all over Europe for whom, in Friedrich Heer's words, "Rome continued to shelter all salvation under her eternal static dome",[17] despite the travails of conscience unleashed by the Modernist controversy of the early 1900's, concerning Biblical inspiration and interpretation. In an Italian context such defiant intransigence is well seen in a leading intellectual, Giovanni Papini. He began as a truculent nihilist with Nietzschean aspirations. Like so many of his kind in early 20th century Italy, where the afterglow of Risorgimento triumph had faded into the light of all too common day, he sought a cause that would focus his passionate spiritual energies. D'Annunzio chose neo-Roman imperialism. Papini seized, in a crushing embrace, Roman Catholicism of the most traditional cast, yet fused the attractions of the papal *Seconda Roma* with elements of the new Rome of the Risorgimento which, for Papini, had under Mussolini issued in a *Terza Roma* ready to revive the hegemony of the old Empire:

> *Fascism is . . . the final struggle for Italian spiritual independence . . . It was not by chance that the metropolis of the universal religion was proclaimed and instituted in the very centre of this earth, which is not only our fatherland, but the fatherland of all those who believe in divine truth and human greatness . . . To the one Emperor there necessarily succeeded the one supreme Pontiff . . . and after the Church was hidden in the depths for three centuries – as was its Founder for three days – behold it broke forth from the deep grave of the catacombs and soared toward the sun by means of the great sky of stone of Michelangelo.*[18]

"The Church soared aloft toward the sun by means of the great sky of stone of Michelangelo." Papini's phrasing fuses the old, sacred,

Catholic Christianity, its temple situated "at the centre of the earth", with the solar religion that was prominent not only in the Roman Empire but in much European tradition of the sacred. There in St Peter's, the high priest or pontifex, successor to Saint Peter, and simulacrum of the original Sacrificial Victim Himself, enacted the rites of a religion that united earth with heaven beneath the Bernini altar suffused by light – that light which was a central symbol of the pagan neo-Platonism which had been incorporated into the mystical doctrines of Catholic Christianity.

The doctrines, rites and festal traditions of *Seconda Roma* were perpetuated throughout the 19th and into the 20th century, until the Second Vatican Council did its best to prune what were deemed excesses, but were among the most potent, if ambiguous, sources of attraction to Protestant and free-thinking visitors from the North who flocked to Rome. *"Che gran belle funzione a sto paese!"*, (What terrific marvellous celebrations this place has!), exclaimed Belli, the Roman dialect poet who both loved and excoriated the grand, squalid paradoxicality of 19th century papal Rome: the daily celebrations all over Rome of the rituals of the cult; the observing of local sacred festivals; the displaying of relics; the visits to the tombs of martyrs; the parades and illuminations – how Romans love light accompanied by noise! – laid on for visiting sovereigns and princes; the ambassadorial presentation of credentials; canonisations with courtly processions of fifty bishops preceding the papal *Sedes Gestatoria*; the choir of five hundred choristers divided among the four sections of the basilica of St Peter's to perform the famous *Tu es Petrus* for four voices – which was also the strong suit of Mustafa, most eminent of castrati.[19]

That there was, to a jaundiced or sceptical eye, something

moribund and unnatural about certain of these ceremonies, comes out in an inimitably malicious account given by Stendhal in the 1820's of an elaborate papal ceremony in St Peter's Piazza:

> At last the great functionaries of the Church arrived, and the Cardinals, heads crowned by pointed caps. Suddenly everyone genuflected, and, on a platform covered by the richest draperies, there appears a figure, pale, inanimate, superb, clad in draperies that reached well above the shoulders, and who to me seemed to form one whole with the altar, the platform and the golden sun before which he was poised in adoration. "You didn't tell me that the Pope was dead", a child nearby said to its mother. And nothing could better have conveyed the total absence of movement in that strange apparition. At such a moment there could only be believers around me, and I too felt so beautifully religious! The Pope's posture is traditional; but since it would be tiresome for an old man, often an invalid, the draperies are so arranged that His Holiness seems to be on his knees, but in fact is seated on a chair . . .[20]

Who can resist Stendhal in that vein! Yet perhaps a fairer impression comes form another, later French free-thinker, Edgar Quinet, in 1836, this time evoking a ceremony inside the Basilica:

> On what is the loftiest expression of the arts, of ruins and of memories, there appears, seated on a throne, a man clad in white. In him all the dead are united, and he is the life and the word in this silent perspective. In front of him kneeling

priests support a book on their shoulders, like the book of
human destiny; he reads from it some lines in a strong
voice. The silence is such that when he closes the book, the
sound of his hand on the page reaches far away. Then,
alone, above that Rome on its knees, he rises to his feet;
extending his arms above the gathering as if to enfold it in
the divine mercy, he utters the familiar words urbi et orbe;
the bells burst forth, the cannon roars, the crowd rises to its
feet. A tumult of pagan enthusiasm rises again from that
exhausted soil; Rome is re-born and lives through the
centuries in that moment. The deserted 'campagna', the
ruins, Hadrian's tomb there next to the Tiber, the multitude
of pilgrims, and, over and above all this, beneath the dome
of Michelangelo, this eternal nameless man, the Pope, the
sole enduring inhabitant and immortal pilgrim of the
Catholic city – there is no-one who is not overwhelmed
forever by such an extraordinary spectacle.[21]

"Rome is re-born and lives through the centuries in that moment."
Quinet's eloquence must surely have echoed half-guiltily in many
a Protestant as well as free-thinking heart, then as now, with
whatever admixture of superciliousness, puritan mistrust, and
covert suspicion of being party to a semi-pagan anachronism. The
whole complex of emotions is there, benignantly responsive yet
tinged with the inevitable irony, in Thackeray's account of Clive
Newcome's visit to St Peter's:

There must be moments, in Rome especially, when every
man of friendly heart, who writes himself English and

Protestant, must feel a pang at thinking that he and his countrymen are insulated from European Christendom. An ocean separates us. From one shore or the other one can see the neighbour cliffs on clear days: one must wish sometimes that there were no stormy gulf between us; and from Canterbury to Rome a pilgrim could pass, and not drown beyond Dover. Of the beautiful parts of the great Mother church I believe among us many people have no idea: we think of lazy friars, of pining cloistered virgins, of ignorant peasants worshipping wood and stones, bought and sold indulgences, absolutions, and the like commonplaces of Protestant satire. Lo! yonder inscription which blazes round the dome of the temple, so great and glorious it looks like heaven almost, and as if the words were written in stars, it proclaims to all the world, that this is Peter, and on this rock the church shall be built, against which Hell shall not prevail. Under the bronze canopy his throne is lit with lights that have been burning before it for ages. Round this stupendous chamber are ranged the grandees of his court. Faith seems to be realized in their marble figures . . . So, you see, at those grand ceremonies which the Roman Church exhibits at Christmas, I looked on as a Protestant. Holy Father on his throne or in his palanquin, cardinals with their tails and their train-bearers, mitred bishops and abbots, regiments of friars and clergy, relics exposed for adoration, columns draped, altars illuminated, incense smoking, organs pealing, and boxes of piping soprani, Swiss guards with slashed breeches and fringed halberts; – between us and all this splendour of old-

world ceremony, there's an ocean flowing: and yonder old statue of Peter might have been Jupiter again, surrounded by a procession of flamens and augurs, and Augustus as Pontifex Maximus, to inspect the sacrifices, – and my feelings at the spectacle had been, doubtless, pretty much the same.[22]

Such a mixture of irony and nostalgia in response to papal Rome was a persistent trait in the Protestant or free-thinker, setting aside the scurrilous viciousness that recurrently beset some of the former. There was the lurking sense that there inhabited the city "characters and symbols so profound that they join the imagery of your own dreams, whose grandeur also is of dreams".[23] There was the hovering suggestion of timelessness lingering around the hint of a paradise not yet quite lost; partly to do with the dream-like splendour of papal ceremonies, partly – in the 19th century at any rate – with the aura of the city itself, where the desolation of transience was omnipresent, yet soothed by the overlay of natural beauty. The Romantic dream of 'timeless' Rome, imperial and papal blended into one, became inescapable for many an artist, scholar, dilettante and simple traveller: a lyrical episode, a pleasing provocation to elegy, a noble exercise in nostalgia, a soul-laden time-warp in an increasingly machine-driven, secular civilisation: – *"Sola Roma resisteva"*,[24] as Silvio Negro put it in his book on *Seconda Roma* between 1850 and 1870.

Let us next dwell on some of the variations of that Romantic and 19th century tradition of feeling about Rome's 'timelessness'; and conclude with an abrupt paradox, a 20th century coda.

Notes to Chapter VI

1. cf., Hugh Honour, *Neo-Classicism* (Penguin, 1968) 175

2. De Tocqueville, *L'Ancien Régime*, tr. M.W. Patterson (Blackwell, 1962) II

3. J.L. Talmon, *Political Messianism, The Romantic Phase* (London, 1960) 22-25

4. Quoted in G. Salvemini, *Mazzini* (Jonathan Cape, 1956) 83-4

5. Quoted in Silvio Negro, *Seconda Rome 1850-1870* (Hoepli, Milano, 1943) 226

6. Hippolyte Taine, *Voyage en Italie* (Paris, 1865) 409 . . . 407

7. B. Croce, *Storia d'Italia dal 1871 al 1915* (Bari, 1966) 175

8. Quoted in Anthony Rhodes, *The Poet as Superman, D'Annunzio* (London, 1959) 144

9. J.L. Talmon, *The Myth of the Nation and the Vision of Revolution* (London, 1980) 476-7 . . . 481

10. Gabriele D'Annunzio, *Elettra*, 'A Roma' (Bologna, 1944) 57

11. Ugo Ojetti, *As They Seemed To Me* (Methuen, 1928) 217-219

12. L. von Ranke, *The History of the Popes*, Vol. II (London, 1907) 537

13. Quoted in H. Daniel-Rops, *The Church in an Age of Revolution 1789-1870* (London and New York, 1965) 241

14. V. Gioberti, *Del Primato Morale e Civile degli Italiani* (3 volumes in one) (Torino, 1920) XI, 104-6 . . . 127

15. cf. H. Daniel-Rops, op. cit., Chapters VII and VIII

16. E.E.Y. Hales, *Pio Nono* (London, 1954) 133

17. F. Heer, *The Intellectual History of Europe* (London, 1953) 312

18. G. Papini, *Italia Mia* (Vallecchi, 1939) 49 . . . 52; *La Scala di Giacobbe* (Vallecchi, 1941) 343

19. Portions of the previous paragraph have been adapted from S. Negro, *Seconda Roma*, 356-7

20. *Rome, Naples et Florence* (Le Divan, Paris) 274-5

21. Quoted in S. Negro, op. cit., 187-8

22. W.M. Thackeray, *The Newcomes* (Oxford University Press) Chapter 35

23. Eleanor Clark, *Rome and a Villa* (London, 1953) 14

24. S. Negro, op. cit., 6. ('Rome alone resisted.')

CHAPTER VII

ERSATZ-ETERNITY
AND
EXISTENTIAL
TIME

19th century responses to Rome in the wake of the Romantic Movement reverse the relation between time and eternity that came to a climax in the Christian-neo-Platonic synthesis of the Baroque period. The cosmos ceased to be a graded descent reflecting more or less beautifully the transcendent One of neo-Platonism, whose rays, fused with the attributes of the Christian deity, were concentrated with special radiance upon the sacred city, Rome. Thereby the city, despite the tokens of transience with which it was littered, was singled out as a special fulcrum of the eternal. By contrast, in the early 19th century, those gigantic wrecks of mankind's constructive genius sublimely scattered amid proliferating natural beauty began to foster the expanding sense of liberation with which the human spirit felt itself imbued in the Romantic period. Humankind, now exultant rather than troubled at the bursting asunder of the closed cosmos, and excited by Piranesian images of purely temporal immensity, discovered in seemingly endless vistas of time and space a symbol of its own infinitude. The latter was most clearly seen in the emergent triumph of industrial technology, and though Romanticism was often hostile to the machine, it shared technology's confidence in endless potentiality, as well as the waxing impulse to transfer primacy from the transcendent to the immanent. Humankind rampant amid the dynamics of time began to take priority over humankind's creaturely function within providential harmonies dependent on a divine source. Writing of the cosmic symbolism of Shelley's Cave of Demogorgon, in *Prometheus Unbound*, Earl Wasserman observes that "the atmosphere enveloping the world is not imposed from without but is the breath exhaled from its core: there is no source of its circumambient condition but its own remote depth".[1]

There had dawned on the human psyche its own power to create, in Starobinski's words, a "universe of sensibility".[2] Expanding sensibility, testing its powers, battened on many forms and shapes. Rome had its special part to play. In some artists and writers of the Romantic period and beyond, the city inspired a surge of noble exaltation. In others, a more lyric string was plucked at the spectacle of such beauty amid such desolation. Most commonly, there was a fusion of the two. In 1819, Shelley, whilst in the throes of composing *Prometheus Unbound*, wrote thus about his wanderings over the Baths of Caracalla, very different in appearance then from the denuded hulk of an abandoned warehouse that they resemble today:

But the most interesting effect remains. In one of the buttresses which supports an immense and lofty arch which 'bridges the very winds of Heaven' are the crumbling remains of an antique winding staircase, whose sides are open in many places to the precipice. This you ascend, and arrive on the summit of these piles. Here grow on every side thick entangled wildernesses of myrtle and the myrtelus and bay and the flowering laurustinus whose white blossoms are just developed, the wild fig and a thousand nameless plants sown by the wandering winds. These woods are intersected on every side by paths, like sheep tracks thro the copse wood of steep mountains, which wind to every part of these immense labyrinths. From the midst rise those pinnacles and masses, themselves like mountains, which have been seen from below. In one place you wind along a narrow strip of weed-grown ruin; on one side is the immensity of earth and sky, on the other, a narrow chasm, which is bounded by an arch of enormous size, fringed by the many coloured foliage and blossoms, and supporting a lofty and irregular pyramid, overgrown like itself by the all-prevailing vegetation. Around rise other crags and other peaks all arrayed and the deformity of their vast desolation softened down by the undecaying investiture of nature. Come to Rome. It is a scene by which expression is overpowered: which words cannot convey.[3]

A sense of potentially endless, and paradisal, regeneration fuses in that passage with the emblems of transience. So too, in the Roman section of Shelley's *Adonais*, "flowering weeds and fragrant copses"[4] dress the mouldering grey ruins of Empire which surround the grave of Keats, "where, like an infant's smile over the dead,/A light of laughing flowers along the grass is spread."[5] *Adonais* ends on a note of energies bursting forth, the mind's thrusting onward, so that even this elegy to Keats, inspired amid ruins and graves, and overtly acknowledging the eternal, was actually fired by the sense of time as dynamic process. The poem is an instance of Rome's ability to amplify and illumine what is endemic to individual sensibility so that as Ehlert, a German traveller of the 19th century wrote, "Rome is innate in each human being, it is like the ideal land of our birth, to which something in us gives allegiance, and from whence we all derive something. Rome tells what is really in one."[6]

"City of the Soul," exclaimed Byron while evoking Rome as stage-setting for the sonorous exaltation of his own ego. While inside St Peter's – the epitome of one aspect of the city's symbolic resonance – he paid tribute to the dome's ability to foster a soul's sense of the infinitude of its own reach and potential: "Till, growing with its growth, we thus dilate/Our spirits to the size of what they contemplate". Earlier Byron had written, of the Coliseum: "There is given/Unto the things of earth, which Time hath bent,/A spirit's feeling . . . Oh, Time! The Beautifier of the dead/Adorner of the ruin . . . ".[7]

Byron, like Shelley at the tomb of Keats, experienced the paradisal desolation which made Rome awaken so gratifying an echo in many a travelling bosom of the 19th century. Its palimpsest of ruins and churches and villas, all scattered amid trees and flowers, mitigated the extremity of transience in one beautiful and sublime symbol, and became a consoling refuge for feelings that might otherwise have been overwhelmed by the increasingly exposed and alienated condition of post-Enlightenment sensibility. In Rome, Nature, Beauty and Death joined hands. "Nature", wrote George Simmel about the charm of ruins, "has used man's work of art as the material for its own creation, just as art had previously taken nature as its raw material. Consequently, the ruin gives an impression of peace, because in it the opposition between these two cosmic powers acts as the soothing image of a purely natural reality."[8]

The city became a quasi-celestial time-warp, an *ersatz*-eternity, for that post-Romantic sensibility which felt at one and the same time alienated, and voluptuously expansive.[9] Rome spoke eloquently and consolingly to its own sense of what was both a predicament and an inspiration: the psyche, exposed and vulnerable to transience, yet buoyed up and harmonised by powers of reflective sentiment. Thus Mme de Staël, through the lips of her blue-stocking vestal, Corinne:

> *Perhaps one of the secret charms of Rome is to reconcile imagination with the long sleep of death. One is resigned for oneself, one suffers less for those one loves . . . The cold and isolation of the tomb beneath that perfect sky, next to so many funerary urns, is less disturbing to the terrified spirit. One thinks oneself waited on by a host of shades, and, from our lonely city to that of the city beneath the transition seems kindly enough.*[10]

Kindred marmoreal sentiments, moonlit on this occasion, inspired Chateaubriand:

> Rome sleeps in the midst of these ruins. That star of the
> night, that globe which one imagines as a globe perished
> and depopulated, casts its own pale solitude over the
> solitudes of Rome; it illumines those empty streets, those
> enclosures, those squares, those gardens where no-one
> enters, monasteries where no cenobite voices are heard, the
> cloister as deserted as the portico of the Coliseum. Pagan
> Rome buries itself deeper and deeper in its tombs, Christian
> Rome descends bit by bit into its catacombs whence it
> emerged.[11]

Chateaubriand, despite his official Catholic zealotry, obviously
took a melancholy satisfaction at the spectacle of Rome's
absorption into all-encompassing cycles of mortality. So too did
Carl Justi who, in mid-19th century, remarked that "all the
grandeurs of the world are buried [in Rome], where time that
destroys and eternity that conserves seem to celebrate their
triumphal rites"[12] In those words Justi also caught perfectly the
quasi-consoling substitution of endless transience for the
metaphysical eternity of an earlier, theological age. "Rome", wrote
Henry Adams in 1860, a young Bostonian, fresh from Germany,
"seemed a pure emotion, quite free of economic or actual values.
No law of progress applied to it. Not even time-sequences – the
last refuge of helpless historians – had value for it." This insight
Adams expands and elaborates: "Rome was a bewildering complex
of ideas, experiments, ambitions, energies; without her, the
Western World was pointless and fragmentary; she gave heart and
unity to it all; yet Gibbon might have gone on for the whole
century, sitting among the ruins of the Capitol, and no one would

have passed, capable of telling him what it meant. Perhaps it meant nothing".[13]

Henry Adams' last remark, with its hint of the nihilistic emanating from Rome, sets one thinking of the moral irony discernible in the city's familiar stance of 'eternity'. Stendhal in the 1820's remarked that "acquaintance with despair accustomed Rome to regard the evils which it endures as inevitable and eternal . . . it knows full well that this particular incarnation of authority will merely be replaced by another, not a whit less evil-minded".[14] Luigi Barzini in mid-20th century wrote in similar vein: "That Italians have been living in the Baroque for the last four centuries can be proved by a cursory examination of all their régimes of the recent past. The 18th century monarchies swept away by Napoleon, the United Kingdom established after the Risorgimento, the veiled dictatorship of the liberal statesmen at the end of the last century and the beginning of this one, the Fascist unconcealed dictatorship, and the Socialist and Catholic combinations ruling today are all specimens of pure Baroque. The names and the officials change. The recipe is always the same".[15] Hence Romans view life as a puppet-theatre, with results confirmed by another mid-20th century observer, Alberto Moravia, who wrote of –

> . . . the unalterable core of Roman 'indifference'. As in 1827, so today, everything that is done and happens in Rome, happens and is done without any real participation on the part of the people . . . With the people of Rome, participation is conditioned and restricted by a deep, yet at the same time discouraging (at least as regards political effects), sense of eternity; hence the all-embracing unreality

> *of life in Rome, which is like a magnificent stage for*
> *performing tragedy, comedy, farce, or plain drama, without*
> *it making any difference.*[16]

At the end of that passage Moravia confronts us with the eternal
Baroque stage-set which constitutes Roman life and art; yet that
very stage-set generates a moral symbolism that is, in some ways,
worthy of respect. Rome, affording as it does a space of
intoxicating scenic grandeur, gives scope for imagination to spread
its wings and to experience, albeit fleetingly, a sense of the spirit's
potential greatness amid the metaphysical and moral void that
modern life has become. Henry James touched on something of
this in his visit to St Peter's in 1873:

> *The soul infinitely expands there, if one will, but all on its*
> *quite human level. It marvels at the reach of our dream and*
> *the immensity of our resources. To be so impressed and put*
> *in our place, we say, is to be sufficiently "saved"; we can't*
> *be more than that in heaven itself; and what specifically*
> *celestial beauty such a show or such a substitute may lack it*
> *makes up for in certainty and tangibility. And yet if one's*
> *hours on the scene are not actually spent in praying, the*
> *spirit seeks it again as for the finer comfort, for the blessing,*
> *exactly, of its example, its protection and its exclusion.*
> *When you are weary of the swarming democracy of your*
> *fellow-tourists, of the unremunerative aspects of human*
> *nature, of Corso and Pincio, of the oppressively frequent*
> *combination of coronets on carriage panels and stupid faces*
> *in carriages, of addled brains and lacquered boots, of ruin*

and dirt and decay, of priests and beggars and takers of
advantage, of the myriad tokens of a halting civilisation, the
image of the great temple depresses the balance of your
doubts, seems to rise above even the highest tide of
vulgarity and make you still believe in the heroic will and
the heroic act. It's a relief, in other words, to feel that
there's nothing but a cab-fare between your pessimism and
one of the greatest of human achievements.[17]

Is the final touch in that passage, about the "cab-fare", a give-away of a side of James himself? Or is it perfectly calculated? At any rate it catches the strain of venality and artifice which tainted that intercourse with the sublime and the eternal which Rome inspired. Nevertheless, down until the fatal era of the 'developers' and the archaeologists, which was about to begin when James wrote, the city still seemed an adequate correlative of the displaced and lingering religiosity of artists, intellectuals and cultivated tourists from the North; provided, as Elizabeth Bowen shrewdly diagnosed, that they were shored up by the saving sense of illusion:

To Rome came the well-to-do in flight from a smoke-greyed
England or raw America: industrialism, soul-killing streets,
top hats.
Romantics, unlike their predecessors of the Age of
Reason, they wished Rome in no way other than as they
found it – over everything shimmered illusion's veil. Days
took on size, from the endlessness of unfrequented ilex
avenues to go driving in, shuttered successions of marble
rooms, the immensity of the churches to be stood in and

galleries to be gazed around, hours of evening by the grey-green river when nothing but distant singing was to be heard, ruins enlarging as the sun sank.[18]

"Over everything shimmered illusion's veil." This was still largely possible until the last two decades of the 19th century. Henry James noted in his later visits to Rome the coarsening and cheapening that others were to enlarge upon *ad nauseam*. This was due mainly to the new buildings, streets and vistas required by the army of bureaucrats that accompanied the Piedmontese Savoy dynasty, when Rome had become the seat of government. For many Romans but, significantly, most of all for foreigners, *le devastazioni dei Piedmontesi*[19] took on an ever-growing momentum of horror. "Rome," lamented Gregorovius, the German historian of the city's Middle Ages, "will lose all its tragic peace." The cherished time-warp was to be rent asunder – and this hurt. Augustus Hare, in his Introduction to the 1903 edition of his *Walks in Rome* – citing from articles in The Times of London – gave anguished and angry attention to the changes. He brooded over "patrician villas destroyed, their casinos dismantled, their beautiful old trees burnt into charcoal". He recoiled from "cheap apartment houses", "hideous new bridges", "gas-works, factories, new streets", "works without harmony, order or governing principles". He concluded that "nothing so pretentious, commonplace, unspiritual and dead had ever been produced as neo-regal Rome".[20] The climax of Hare's abuse took the form of a quotation from D'Annunzio: "On these patrician lawns where, only the previous spring, the violets had blossomed more numberless than the blades of grass, were now mounds of lime, heaps of brick, the wheels of stone-laden cars creaked on the turf, on the air were the oaths of the drivers, the shout of the overseers, while every hour hastened the brutal work which was to efface and occupy the sacred soil once dedicated to Beauty and to Dreams".

D'Annunzio was a far greater and more varied writer than allowed by his Anglo-Saxon reputation, which dismisses him as a proto-fascist playboy with a swollen libido. As well as glorifying the 'Third Rome' of the Risorgimento, D'Annunzio also gave us an appalled foretaste of the modernised city of the 20th century, a kind of imaginative extension of Piranesi's *I Carceri*: monstrous, de-centred spaces dotted with isolated hominids:

> *With matlock and trowel – and fraud – as the instruments, from one week to the next, with nightmarish rapidity, on foundations filled with rubble, there arose enormous empty cages, riddled with rectangular openings, surmounted by sham entablatures, encrusted with repulsive plaster-work. A kind of immense whitish tumour protruded from the sides of the old city, and sucked its life . . . I hear again behind me the screeching of the electric tram on its rails . . . I know the wound incised in the fated street by the glittering steel rails and inflicted on eyes of desperation lost in that suffocating air. I know you well, torrid days, deadly noons, nerve-ridden encounters of haggard, exhausted faces, 'road closed' amid walls like furnaces, silent burnt-out squares, unyielding asphalt, red-hot paving-stones . . . There come back to me certain Roman afternoons . . . there come back to me something of that desperation, that nausea . . .* [21]

217

An aesthete of a later generation, English this time, and a doughty preserver of ancient edifices in his own country, tells a similar tale. James Lees-Milne wrote in 1956 of the spirit of a whole city's being altered "from a feathery wilderness of ineffable beauty to a rubbish-dump under a net-work of wires – the aqueducts screened by electric pylons, and long before you reach the Porta del Popolo the sheep have been replaced by flocks of glossy advertisements of Chlorodont and Vov, nibbling their way into Mussolini's cement suburbs".[22] Mussolini, as well as being the partly evil genius of modern Italy as a nation, was also the disastrous impresario mainly responsible for those desolate spaces that sliced up the old city into archaeological sites. "Archaeology", Eleanor Clark reminds us, "was helped by fascism – but it would only have gone ahead more slowly without it. The past, like love, was never so precarious and abused and useless; it was never so thoroughly investigated . . . Imagination has been killed; a strange air of the hygienic takes its place . . . the question is of the survival of the imagination under any system in this century."[23]

Rome, from having been the archetypal image for the 19th and even the early 20th century traveller, of a paradise not quite lost, has become a place whose time-defying monumentality only exacerbates the angst of the post-Christian consciousness. This is induced by the sense of "nausea" – D'Annunzio's word – aroused by the mechanised void of the modern megalopolis. The Void, – *le Néant* – *Angst,* Nausea: these are 1940's and 1950's words, implying the sense of a contingent and de-centred self trapped in the purposeless flux of time. Such, shorn of subtle opacities, was the bequest of Heidegger to the Existentialists. The words became part of the intellectual baggage, frequently pretentious, of many a literary cosmopolite. Yet even Eleanor Clark, who wrote one of the most original and least fashion-prone books about Rome in that same post-World War Two period, echoed the mood. The palimpsest quality of Rome – "the compounds of Time" – had ceased to generate a pleasing melancholy, an aesthetic cloning of the eternal, and become a source of nightmare:

> *The Angst is going to get a lot worse . . . there are the mess and the blazing sun, the incongruity, the too-muchness of everything . . . acres of ruin, some handsome, some shabby lumps and dumps of shapeless masonry, sprinkled through acres of howling modernity – an impossible compounding of Time, in which no century has respect for any other, and all hit you in a jumble at every turn . . . where spaces open out and close up before you suddenly as in dreams . . . a place beautiful at certain points, at certain moments, but closed to you, repellent, where you are always being reminded of something, you cannot tell what, but it is like the fear of falling down a great well.[24]*

Only a defiantly loyal Romanophile of the late 20th century would deny the force of these intimations, these exacerbations . . . It is Time that has now taken over as the primary symbol of Rome; random yet mechanised time, far more afflicting to the spirit than the majestic time-shadowed solitudes of Piranesi. Yet, still predominant, are the accumulated facades, vaults, and gesticulating figures of what is still a Baroque city. How do they mesh with existentialist, post-Heideggerian desolation?

Very neatly, if one takes the view of the great modern Italian poet, Ungaretti. For Ungaretti, the Baroque by its over-assertive externality and floridity epitomised the sense of the existential Void. But then there is the countervailing intuition of a major French poet and cultural historian, Yves Bonnefoy. For him Baroque may at its finest be the aesthetic style best capable of rendering an authentic sense of the sacred for the religious consciousness of the modern age. This has much to do with the fact that the modern age has lost the sense of a static Eternity overarching and circumscribing the transient, in the manner implied by both pagan and Christian neo-Platonism. "Life" in the words of a writer on the Spanish Baroque,[25] "is of necessity a failure when it is the attempt to make of the Time-Object a Spatial-Object". That was why the old cosmological, neo-Platonised Christianity, welded to ideals of harmony and unity, that flourished in one guise or another down to the Renaissance, reached an impasse in the 17th century: the age of dynamics and the open, uncircumscribed cosmos. The 17th century Baroque was in certain respects a culmination of the more ancient tradition, which achieved an exotic apotheosis in the grandiose *Summae* of Athanasius Kircher, and in the pretence on the part of the Roman Church of perpetuating the imperial dream of a sacred, central city within a closed cosmos. Yet behind the surviving visual panoply of that Baroque synthesis Ungaretti perceived – the Void, *Il Vuoto.* The Baroque also, however – so Yves Bonnefoy stresses – exposed itself to an extreme perception of transience and illusion and, by its paradoxical manner of doing so, encapsulated a sense of the sacred more authentic than much of what preceded it.

The seemingly opposed yet reciprocal intuitions of Ungaretti and Bonnefoy may help us to focus the paradox implicit in the

Baroque, and thereby to glimpse a still abiding centrality, as religious symbol in the modern age, of Rome, city of the Baroque.

Ungaretti, after a childhood in Alexandria, frequented Parisian avant-garde circles, especially the one around Apollinaire, and found fame by writing terse, 'Imagist' poems about his experience as a young soldier in the First World War. When he first came to live in Rome in the 1920's he set about writing sequences of short lyrics called, very pertinently, *Sentimiento del Tempo* (The Feeling of Time). They are hermetic in style, intensely personal, and do not in any obvious way evoke the city of Rome. Yet Rome, so Ungaretti's essays tell us, was intensely felt by him throughout that period, both as presence and symbol; and it was from Baroque Rome that he derived his own special intuition of the city's nature: "In Rome, one has a feeling of emptiness. It is natural, when one has a feeling for the void, that one can't help equally possessing a horror of the void. These piled-up ruins brought from everywhere, in order not to leave the tiniest fragment of space, to fill everything up, to leave nothing, nothing free. The horror of the void one can feel infinitely more in Rome than in the desert even, or in any other part of the world."[26]

The Baroque, Ungaretti proceeds, juxtaposed everywhere in Rome to the bric-à-brac of ancient ruins, induces an acute sense of gratuitousness, of purposelessness; the excess and exuberance of the Baroque is one of humanity's most explosive efforts at filling the void with the maximum sense of its own highly dramatised presence. Yet that very drama and excess were the symptoms of a world which had lost the sense of Being, and of the Divine as an encompassing presence. It compensated by providing an overdose of power-laden images – "it was the Baroque which invented the escapist spirit by teaching us to cherish the exotic" – by a frenzy of vibrant and fleeting gesture, and by structures whose very monumentality had an element of 'surplusage' that betokened a sense of the Void. "Michelangelo," – Ungaretti has a disconcerting tendency to take Michelangelo as his touchstone of the Baroque – "and a few others from the end of the 15th till the 18th century had, in Italy, that feeling, a feeling of horror of the Void, that is of horror of a world deprived of God."[27]

Yves Bonnefoy, whose views on the Baroque take him in a different direction, doubtless would not dispute a good deal of what Ungaretti says, and which indeed, though filtered through Ungaretti's very individual perceptions, is not startlingly original. Bonnefoy, however, has turned the whole response to the Baroque on its head. To take at face value the densely proliferating gestures and, in particular, the theatricality and illusionism of the Baroque, is, he believes, to miss a crucial point. In what sense, Bonnefoy asks, could Baroque phantasy, gesture and theatricality be intended to deceive? And answers: the Baroque, by conveying a maximum of externality through its gesturing histrionics, implies that its manipulations of appearance are – just that, and no more. Thus, paradoxically, by its very candid consciousness of illusion, it betrays an openness to the sacred that is lacking in the more self- contained, geometric harmonies of Renaissance spatiality. Bonnefoy is worth quoting at some length on these matters:

> *If there is theatricality in those grand,* outré *gestures of the Baroque is there not also ambiguity? Does not the Baroque, by a reverse movement, abolish all that cumbersome*

exteriority? . . . *By its excessiveness it is supposed to portend the presence of the divine, but that excessiveness announces itself by such externality of gesture as to constitute an avowal – like the oscillating and self-cancelling décor of Baroque vaults – that it is simply an image; our joy consists in seeing that appearance is illusion – and by that very fact conveying the nearness of the sacred. So too with the theatre, when not degraded: the puppet openly proclaims itself wood and rags. By the very fact [of avowed illusoriness] the Baroque opposes no obstacle to the shining forth of a presence, a presence with which our contact* – which is always fussed by proofs – *is re-established. In sum: the Baroque is not a* trompe l'oeil, *but the rendering of Being by means of illusion, and its eloquence proclaims that illusion in the very instant of creation – thus touching the invisible. Despite its high degree of visibility the Baroque bears on the interior experience of Grace. It is the route to the invisible – which does not mean that there are not remnants of externality in its attempted synthesis. Form in Bernini has still its beauty; indeed he drew much on Renaissance elaborateness, to such an extent that he is sometimes claimed as the inheritor of classicism. But that beauty of his is not the unstable evocation of an inaccessible essence, it is a simple moment of reality in its immediacy . . . What concerns Bernini is not the object in itself, but our relation to it, the image of an encounter. Bernini has effected the transposition from the visible – that trap – to the existential.*[28]

223

Bonnefoy's perceptions are subtle, elusive, and dazzlingly imaginative. Yet they do endow elements of Baroque style and sensibility – and hence, the Baroque city of Rome – with an unexpectedly moving relevance to the religious consciousness of the late 20th century. In this perspective Rome becomes not the city of Eternity – "Eternity, the largest of the idols, the mightiest of the rivals of God", as Chesterton wrote, but the city of Time, of existential Time.

All along there had been, amidst the classical and Renaissance values that the Baroque style in Rome brought to an effulgent climax, a saving ambiguity. An intensely visual culture wrought to its highest pitch; an extravagant theatricality amidst divine things; a potent espousal of its own illusoriness: all this was oblique testimony to Baroque awareness that its realm was, and could only be, a realm of appearance. Then, as now, an intoxicating flourish of self-abnegating illusion is perhaps the most fitting tribute that mankind can offer to the *Deus Absconditus*, the Hidden God.

Notes to Chapter VII

1. Earl Wasserman, *Shelley's Prometheus Unbound* (Johns Hopkins Press, 1975) 152

2. J. Starobinski, *The Invention of Liberty* (Skira, 1964) 206

3. *The Letters of P.B. Shelley, II, Shelley in Italy*, ed. F.L. Jones (OUP, 1964) 495

4. P. B. Shelley, *Adonais*, stanza 49, line 435

5. ibid., lines 440-I

6. Louis Ehlert quoted in Silvio Negro, *Seconda Roma* (Milano, 1943) 24

7. Byron, *Childe Harold's Pilgrimage*, Canto IV, st. 158 . . . st. 129-30

8. Quoted in Starobinski, op.cit., 180

9. cf. Starobinski, op. cit., 206

10. Mme de Stael, *Corinne* (Paris, n. d.) 35-6 ('Improvisation de Corinne au Capitole')

11. A. de Chateaubriand, *Oeuvres Complétes* Vol. 6, 'Promenade dans Rome, (Garnier, Paris) 292-3

12. Quoted in Silvio Negro, op. cit., 249

13. *The Education of Henry Adams* (London, 1928) 90 . . . 91 . . . 93

14. Quoted in J. McGann, *The Beauty of Inflections* (Oxford, 1985) 329

15. L. Barzini, *The Italians* (New York, 1965) 329

16. Quoted in McGann, op. cit., 331-2

17. Henry James, *Italian Hours* (Evergreen Edition, Grove Press, New York, 1959) 151-2

18. E. Bowen, *A Time in Rome* (Penguin Books, 1989) 108

19. Quoted in Silvio Negro, op. cit., 14

20. A. Hare, *Walks in Rome*, Vol. I, (London and New York, 1903) 11-12

21. G. D'Annunzio, *Libro Primo, Maia, Laus Vitae*, ed. E. Palmieri (Zanichelli Editore, Bologna, 1949) 374-6. (The notes to this edition refer to scattered sections of D'Annunzio's prose in similar vein, which I have interlaced with bits of the poetry from *Maia*. The opening section, on the building horrors of the "Third Rome", comes from *Le Vergini delle Rocce*.)

22. J. Lees-Milne, *Roman Mornings* (London, 1956) XIII

23. Eleanor Clark, *Rome and a Villa* (Michael Joseph, 1953) 90-1

24. ibid., 17

25. Arland Ussher, *Spanish Mercy* (Gollancz, 1959) 49

26. Quoted in F.C. Jones, *Ungaretti* (Edinburgh University Press) 15

27. ibid., 47

28. Y. Bonnefoy, *Rome 1630* (Flammarion, 1970) 38-40 . . . 37 . . . 17

BIBLIOGRAPHY

Adams, Henry | *The Education of Henry Adams*, London, 1928

Adams, R M | *The Roman Stamp*, University of California Press, 1974

Allers, R | 'Microcosmos', Traditio, II, 1944

Anderson, J F | *Introduction to the Metaphysics of St Thomas Aquinas*, Regnery, 1953

Ariès, P | *The Hour of Our Death*, Penguin Books, 1983

Arnou R | 'Platonisme des Pères' in *Dictionnaire de Théologie Catholique (XII)*

Auerbach, E | 'Figura', *Scenes from the Drama of European Literature*, Meridian Books, 1959

Balthasar, Hans Urs von | *La Gloire et La Croix: Le Domaine de la Métaphysique: Les Constructions*, Aubier, 1982

Barth, Hans | 'Das Zeitalter des Barocks und die Philosophie von Leibniz', *Die Kunsttormen des Barockzeitalters*, Bern, 1956

Barzini, L | *The Italians*, New York, 1965

Battisti, E	*Rinascimento e Barocco,* Einaudi, 1960
Bettagno E (ed.)	*Piranesi Tra Venezia e Europa,* Firenze, 1983
Binkley, R C	*Realism and Nationalism 1852–1871,* New York, 1935
Blumenberg, H	*The Legitimacy of the Modern Age,* MIT Press, 1983
Blunt, A	*Borromini,* Allen Lane, 1979
Bonnefoy, Yves	*Rome 1630,* Flammarion, Paris, 1970
Borst, A	*Der Turmbau von Babel,* Stuttgart, 1963
Bossuet, J-B	*Sermons* (II), Garnier, Paris
Bossuet, J-B	*Oraisons Funèbres,* Garnier, Paris
Bouyer, L	*The Spirituality of the New Testament and the Fathers,* Burns and Oates, 1963
Bowen, E	*A Time in Rome,* Penguin Books, 1989
Brentano, Robert	*Rome Before Avignon,* Longman, 1974
Bruyne, E de	*Études d'Esthétique Mediéval,* Brugge, 1946
Buffon, J	*Oeuvres Complètes,* Paris, 1857
Callahan, J F	*Four Views of Time in Ancient Philosophy,* Connecticut, 1979
Calvesi, Maurizio	'Ideologia e Riferimenti delle "Carceri"', in *Piranesi tra Venezia e L'Europa,* a cura di E Bettagno, Firenze, 1983
Calvesi, Maurizio	Introduction to Italian Translation of H Focillon's *G B Piranesi,* Bologna, 1967
Cassirer, E	*The Individual and the Cosmos in Renaissance Philosophy,* Blackwell, 1963
Chadwick, Owen	*The Popes and the European Revolution,* OUP, 1981

Charpentrat, Pierre	'Remarques sur la Structure de L'Espace Baroque', *Nouvelle Revue Française*, August, 1961
Chastel, A	'Le Baroque et la Mort', *Retorica e Barocco: Atti del III Congresso Internazionale di Studi Umanistici*, June, 1954
Chateaubriand, A de	*Oeuvres Complètes Volume 6, 'Promenade dans Rome'*, Garnier, Paris, 1929-1938
Chenu, M-D	*Nature, Man and Society in the Twelfth Century*, Chicago and London, 1968
Clark, Eleanor	*Rome and a Villa*, Michael Joseph, 1953
Cochrane, C N	*Christianity and Classical Culture*, OUP, 1957
Copleston, F	*History of Philosophy*, Volume III, London, 1964
Crashaw, Richard	*The Poems, English, Latin and Greek*, ed. L C Martin, Oxford, 1927
Croce, B	*Storia d'Italia dal 1871 al 1915*, Bari, 1966
Cusa, Nicholas of	*On Learned Ignorance*, tr. G Heron, Routledge and Kegan Paul, 1954
D'Annunzio, G	*Libro Primo, Maia, Laus Vitae*, ed. E Palmieri, Zanichelli Editore, Bologna, 1949
D'Annunzio, G	*Elettra*, Zanichelli Editore, Bologna, 1944
Daniel-Rops, H	*The Church in an Age of Revolution 1789–1870*, London and New York, 1965
Davis, C T	*Dante and the Idea of Rome*, OUP, 1957
de Santillana, G	*The Crime of Galileo*, Heinemann, 1958
De Vries, G W	*Piranesi an het idee van de Prachtige stad*, 1001 Amsterdam, 1990

Dell 'Arco, Fagiolo,

M e M   *Bernini, una Introduzione al Gran Teatro del Barocco,* Roma, 1967

Dell 'Arco, Fagiolo,

M, e Carrandini, S   *L'Effimero Barocco,* Roma, 1978

Diderot, D   *Lettre sur les Aveugles,* Textes Littéraires Francais, Droz, 1951

Dilliston, F W   *Christianity and Symbolism,* London, 1955

Eco, Umberto   *The Aesthetics of St Thomas Aquinas,* Radius, USA, 1988

Einem, H von   'Bemerkungen zur Cathedra Petri des Lorenzo Bernini', *Nachrichten der Akademie der Wissenschaften in Gottingen,* 4, 1955

Eitner, Lorenz   'Cages, Prisons and Captives in 18th Century Art' *Images of Romanticism,* Yale University Press, 1978

Eliade, M   'Psychologie et Histoire des Religions – à propos du Symbolisme du "Centre"', *Eranos Jahrbuch,* Band XIX, 1950

Eliade, M   *Cosmos and History,* Harper Torch Books, 1959

Evans, R J W   *The Making of the Hapsburg Monarchy,* OUP, 1979

Fabre, J   *Lumières et Romantisme,* C Klincksieck, Paris, 1963

Fleming, John   *Robert Adam and his Circle in Edinburgh and London,* London, 1962

Focillon, H   *G B Piranesi, 1720–1778,* Paris, 1918

Fumaroli, M   *L'Age d'Eloquence,* Droz, 1980

Gandillac, M de   'Sur la Sphère Infinie de Pascal', *Revue de l'Histoire de la Philosophie*, Jan–Mars, 1943

Gandillac, M de   'Pascal et le Silence du Monde', in *Blaise Pascal: L'Homme et l'Oeuvre*, Les Editions de Minuit, 1950

Garin, E ed.   *Pico della Mirandola*, Valecchi Editore, 1942

Gioberti, V   *Del Primato Morale e Civile degli Italiani*, 3 volumes in one, Torino, 1920

Godwin, J   *Music, Mysticism and Magic*, Arkana, 1986

Godwin, J   *Athanasius Kircher*, Thames and Hudson Ltd, 1979

Gracián, B   *El Criticón*, Editorial Planeta, 1985

Grant, Edward   *Much Ado About Nothing, Theories of Space and Vacuum from the Middle Ages to the Scientific Revolution*, OUP, 1981

Gryphius, J   *Gedichte*, Reclam, 1968

Hales, E E Y   *Pio Nono*, London, 1954

Hare, A   *Walks in Rome*, London & New York, 1903

Harries, K   'The Infinite Sphere', *Journal of the History of Philosophy*, 13–14, 1976

Heer, F   *The Intellectual History of Europe*, Weidenfeld and Nicolson, 1966

Heidegger, M   *Being and Time*, Harper and Row, 1962

Heninger, S K   *Touches of Sweet Harmony*, San Marino, California, 1974

Holmes, G   *Dante*, OUP, 1980

Honour, Hugh   *Neo-Classicism*, Penguin, 1968

231

Hook, J	'Urban VIII, the Paradox of a Spiritual Monarchy', *The Courts of Europe*, ed. A G Dickens, Thames and Hudson, 1977
Huse, N	'La Fontaine des Fleuves du Bernini', *Revue de L'Art*, (7), 1970
Innocent III, Pope	Sermon XXI, Migne, *Patrologia Latina*, CCXVII
Iversen, E	*Obleisks in Exile: The Obelisks of Rome*, Copenhagen, 1968
James, Henry	*Italian Hours*, Evergreen Edition, Grove Press, New York, 1959
Jaspers, K	*Nikolaus Cusanus*, München, 1964
Jones, F C	*Ungaretti*, Edinburgh University Press, 1977
Justi, C	*Winckelmann und Seine Zeitgenossen*, Band 2, Phaidon Verlag, Köln, 1956
Kauffmann, Hans	*G L Bernini, Die Figürlichen Kompositionen*, Berlin, Gebr. Mann Verlag, 1970
Kaufmann, E	*Architecture in the Age of Reason*, Dover Books, 1967
Keyser, E de	*The Romantic West 1789–1850*, Skira, 1965
Kircher, A	*Turris Babel*, Amstelodami, 1679
Kircher, A	*Arca Noe*, Amstelodami, 1675
Kircher, A	*Musurgia Univeralis*, Romae, 1660
Kircher, A	*Iter Ecstaticum Coeleste*, Nuremberg, 1660 (This is a later edition of the *Itinerarium Ecstaticum* published in Rome in 1656. References in the text are to the Nuremberg edition).
Kircher, A	*Oedipus Aegyptiacus*, Romae, 1652–4
Kircher, A	*Ars Magna Lucis et Umbrae*, Romae, 1646

Kircher, A	*Obeliscus Pamphilius*, Romae, 1650
Kircher, A	*Arithmologia*, Romae, 1665
Kitao, T	*The Circle and the Oval in the Square of St Peter's*, New York, 1974
Klingner, F	'Roms Als Idee', *Antike 29*, 1927
Koyré, A	*From the Closed World to the Infinite Universe*, Johns Hopkins Press, 1957
Kuntz, Paul G	'The Hierarchical Vision of St Roberto Bellarmino', in *Jacob's Ladder and the Tree of Life: Concepts of Hierarchy and the Great Chain of Being*, Bern and New York, 1986
Lavin, Irving	*Bernini and the Crossing of St Peter's*, New York University Press, 1968
Lavin, I (ed.)	*G–L Bernini: New Aspects of his Life and Thought*, Pennsylvania State University Press, 1985
Lechner, G S	'Tommaso Campanella and Andrea Sacchi's Fresco of Divina Sapienza in the Palazzo Barberini', *The Art Bulletin*, Volume LVIII (1) 1976
Lees–Milne, J	*Roman Mornings*, London, 1956
Lees–Milne, J	*Saint Peter's*, London, 1967
Legrand, J G	'Notice sur la Vie et les Ouvrages de G–B Piranesi' reprinted in *Nouvelles de L'Estampe*, no. 5, 1969
Lehmann, Karl	'Piranesi as Interpreter of Roman Architecture', *Smith College Museum of Art*, Northampton, Mass., 1961
Leibniz, G W	*Confessio Philosophi*, Frankfurt–am–Main, 1967

Leibniz, G W   *The Monadology* etc. tr. R Latta, OUP, 1951

Lenoble, R   *Mersenne, ou la Naissance du Mécanisme,* Paris, 1943

Lubac, H de   *Pic de la Mirandole,* Aubier, 1974

MacDonald, W L   *Piranesi's Carceri: Sources of Invention,* Northampton, 1979

Mahnke, D   *Unendliche Sphäre und Allmittelpunkt,* Halle, 1937

Mâle, E   *L'Art Réligieux de la fin du XVIe Siècle, du XVIIe Siècle et du XVIIIe Siècle,* Paris, 1951

Maphaei, S R E   Card. nunc Urbani Papae VIII, *Poemata,* 1630

Marino, G B   *Dicerie Sacre e la Strage degl Innocenti,* A cura di G Pozzi, Turin: Einaudi, 1960

Martin, J R   *Baroque,* Harper and Row, 1977

McGann, J   *The Beauty of Inflections,* Oxford, 1985

McGinness, F J   'The Rhetoric of Praise and the New Rome of the Counter Reformation', *Rome in the Renaissance: the City and the Myth,* Binghampton, NY, 1982

Michel, P–H   'La Querelle du Géocentrisme', *Studi Secenteschi (2)* 1961

Momigliano, A   'Ancient History and the Antiquarian', *Journal of the Warburg and Courtauld Institute,* 13–14, 1950–1

Moore, F G   'On Urbs Aeterna and Urbs Sacra', *Transactions of the American Philological Association,* XXV, 1894

Moravia, A   *L'Uomo Como Fine,* Bompiani, 1964

Moreau, J   *L'Idée d'Univers dans la Pensée Antique,* SEI, Torino, 1953

Müller, W	*Die Heilige Stadt,* Stuttgart, 1961
Negro, Silvio	*Seconda Roma 1850–1870,* Hoepli, Milano, 1943
Ogetti, Ugo	*As They Seemed To Me,* Methuen, 1928
O'Malley, J	*Giles of Viterbo on Church and Reform,* Leiden, 1968
Oliver, J H	'The Ruling Power', *Transactions of the American Philosophical Society,* New Series, Volume 43 (4) 1953
Ost, H	'Borromini's Römische Universitätskirche San Ivo alla Sapienza', *Zeitschrift für Kunstgeschichte,* XX, 1967
Panofsky, E	*Symbolic Images,* Phaidon, 1978
Panofsky, E	*Galileo as Critic of the Arts,* Nijhoff, The Hague, 1954
Panofsky, E	*Tomb Sculpture,* Thames and Hudson, 1964
Panofsky, E	'Mors Testimonium Vitae', *Studien Zur Toskanischen Kunst,* ed. W Lotz, München, 1964
Papini, G	*Italia Mia,* Vallecchi, 1939, *La Scala di Giacobbe,* Vallecchi, 1941
Paschoud, F	*Roma Aeterna,* Institut Suisse de Rome, 1967
Pastor, L	*History of the Popes,* Volume XXVII, tr. E Graf, London, 1938
Pastine, D	*La Nascita dell Idolatria,* Firenze, 1978
Pemble, J	*The Mediterranean Passion, Victorians and Edwardians in the South,* Oxford, 1987
Petersson, R J	*The Art of Ecstasy,* London, 1970
Plotinus	*The Enneads,* tr. S McKenna, Faber, 1969

Pochat, G	'Über Berninis "Concetto" zum Vierströmbrunnen auf Piazza Navona', *Konsthistorik Tidskrift* (35) 1966
Portoghesi, P	*Roma Barocca,* MIT Press, 1970
Poulet, Georges	'Piranèse et les Poètes Romantiques Français', *Nouvelle Revue Francaise,* Volume 13, 160, 1966
Poulet, G	'Les Prisons Imaginaires de Piranèse', *Nouvelle Revue Francaise* Volume 9, 67, 1961
Poulet, G	*The Metamorphoses of the Circle,* Johns Hopkins Press, 1966
Pratt, K J	'Rome as Eternal' *J H I,* 26, 1965
Praz, Mario	*On Neo–Classicism,* Thames and Hudson, 1969
Praz, Mario	*G B Piranesi, I Carceri,* Rizzoli, 1975
Preimesberger, R	'Pignus Imperii: Ein Beitrag zu Berninis Aeneasgruppe', *Festschrift Wolfgang Braunfels* ed. F Piel and J Traeger, Tübingen, 1977
Preimesberger, R	'Obeliscus Pamphilius', *Münchner Jahrbuch für Kunstgeschichte,* 3rd Series, Volume XXV, 1974
Preimesberger, R	'Pontifex Romanus per Aeneam Praesignatus', *Römisches Jahrbuch für Kunstgeschichte* (16) 1976
Prey, P de la Ruffiniére du	'Solomonic Symbolism in Borromini's Church of San Ivo della Sapienza' in *Zeitschrift für Kunstgeschichte,* XXXI, 1968
Prudentius	*Contra Symmachum,* tr. H J Thomson, Heinemann Ltd, 1949
Raimondi, E	*Letteratura Barocca,* Firenze, 1961

Ranke, L von   *The History of the Popes,* London, 1907

Reeves, M   *Joachim of Flora and the Prophetic Future,*
                           SPCK, 1976

Reilly, P Conor, S J   *Athanasius Kircher S J, Master of a Hundred
                           Arts,* Wiesbaden–Rom, 1974

Rhodes, Anthony   *The Poet as Superman, D'Annunzio,* London,
                           1959

Rivosecchi, V   *Esotismo a Roma Barocca,* Bulzoni Editore,
                           1982

Robinson, D S (ed.)   *Anthology of Modern Philosophy,* New York,
                           1931

Rochetta, G Incisa della   *L'Arte,* Volume XXVII (2–3) 64

Roques, R   *L'Univers Dionysien,* Aubier, 1954

Rorem, P (ed.) tr. C
     Luibheid   *Pseudo–Dionysius, The Complete Works,*
                           Paulist Press, 1987

Rosenblum, R   *Transformations in Late Eighteenth Century Art,*
                           Princeton University Press, 1974

Rossi, P   *The Dark Abyss of Time,* Chicago and London,
                           1984

Roston, M   *Milton and the Baroque,* Macmillan, 1980

Rousset, J   'Saint–Yves et les Poètes', in *L'Intérieur et
                           L'Extérieur,* J. Corti, Paris, 1976

Salvemini, G   *Mazzini,* Jonathan Cape, 1956

Santillana, G de   *The Crime of Galileo,* Heinemann, 1958

Schenk, H G   *The Mind of the European Romantics,* OUP,
                           1979

Scott, Jonathan   *Piranesi,* London & New York, 1975

Sedlmayr, Hans	*Art in Crisis,* London, 1957
Shelley, P B	*The Letters of P B Shelley II, Shelley in Italy,* ed. F L Jones, OUP, 1964
Sherard, Philip	*The Eclipse of Man and Nature,* Lindisfarne Press, 1987
Shumaker, W	*Occult Sciences in the Renaissance,* Berkeley, California, 1972
Simson, O von	*The Gothic Cathedral,* Princeton University Press, 1974
Singleton, C S tr. and ed.	*The Divine Comedy,* Princeton, 1975
Skrine, P	*The Baroque,* Methuen & Co, 1978
Souiller, D	*La Littérature Baroque en Europe,* Presses Universitaires de France, 1988
Spenser, E	*Poetical Works,* OUP, 1952
Spitzer, L	*Essays on 17th Century French Literature,* OUP, 1983
St Augustine	Epistle CLXXXVIII
St Leo the Great	Sermon LXXXII, Migne, *Patrologia Latina LIV*
St Leo the Great	Sermon LXXXIII, Migne, *Patrologia Latina LIV*
Staël, Mme de	*Corinne,* Paris, n.d.
Starobinski, J	*The Invention of Liberty,* Skira, 1964
Stefani, G	*Musica Barocca,* Bompiani, 1974
Stendhal	*Rome, Naples et Florence,* Le Divan, Paris, 1927
Stinger, C L	*The Renaissance in Rome,* Indiana University Press, 1985
Stock, B	*Myth and Science in the 12th Century,* Princeton, 1972

Tafuri, M	'Borromini e Piranesi: La Città come "Ordine Infranto"' in *Piranesi: tra Venezia e l'Europe,* a cura di A Bettagno, Firenze, 1983
Tafuri, Manfredo	*The Sphere and the Labyrinth,* MIT Press, 1987
Taine, Hippolyte	*Voyage en Italie,* Paris, 1865
Talmon, J L	*The Myth of the Nation and the Vision of Revolution,* London, 1980
Talmon, J L	*Political Messianism, The Romantic Phase,* London, 1960
Tetius, G	*Aedes Barberinae,* Romae, 1642
Thackeray, W M	*The Newcomes,* Oxford University Press
Tuzet, H	*Le Cosmos et l'Imagination,* J Corti, Paris, 1963
Ungaretti, G	*Saggi e Interventi,* Mondadori, 1974
Ussher, Arland	*Spanish Mercy,* Gollancz, 1959
Viatte, J	*Les Sources Occultes du Romantisme,* Paris, 1928
Wasserman, Earl	*Shelley's Prometheus Unbound,* Johns Hopkins Press, 1975
Weil, M S	'The Devotion of the Forty Hours and Roman Baroque Illusion', *Journal of the Warburg and Courtauld Institute,* 37, 1974
Whitman, J	*Allegory,* OUP, 1987
Wilton–Ely, J	'Utopia or Megalopolis? The "Ichnographia" of Piranesi's "Campus Martius" Reconsidered', *Piranesi tra Venezia e l'Europa,* a cura di E Bettagno, Firenze, 1983
Wilton–Ely, J	*The Mind and Art of G B Piranesi,* Thames and Hudson, London, 1978

Wilton–Ely, J (ed.) — *G B Piranesi: The Polemical Works,* Gregg International Publishers Ltd, 1972

Wittkower, R — *Art and Architecture in Italy 1600–1750,* Penguin Books, 1973

Wittkower, R — *Gian–Lorenzo Bernini, the Sculptor of the Roman Baroque,* 3rd edition, Phaidon, Oxford, 1981

Wittkower R and I B Jaffe — *Baroque Art: the Jesuit Contribution,* New York, 1972

Yates, F — *Giordano Bruno and the Hermetic Tradition,* RKP, 1964

INDEX

Suger, Abbot, 57

Sylvestris, Bernardus, *Cosmographia*, 57

Symmachus, 94

Tafuri, Manfredo, 151, 180

Taine, Hippolyte, 193

Talmon, J.L., 190, 191, 194-95

Tasso, T., *Il Mondo Creato*, 70

Teresa, St, Bernini's sculpture of, 130

Tetius, 42-3, 147

Tetragrammaton, 51

Thackeray, W.M., Clive Newcome's reaction to St Peter's, 202-04

Thomson, James, *The Seasons*, 178

Time, 162-170 passim, 173, 190, 191, 208, 210, 218, 219, 224; dynamics of, 208, 210; expansion of, 162-173 passim; Existential Time, 224; meaningless flux of, 218, 219; as Progress, 190, 191

Tocqueville, A. de, 189

Tower of Babel, 33, 138

Trajan, Baths of, 173

Trent, Council of, 24

Triads, 53

Tridentine Church, post-, see also Counter-Reformation, 24, 88, 98

Tripoli, 19

Trismegistus, Hermes, a mythical ancient Egyptian seer whose name was linked to various neo-Platonic writings known as *Corpus Hermeticum*, q.v., 27, 32, 33, 53, 64-5; as one of *Prisci Theologi*, 64

Triumphalism, papal, 98-102 passim, 105

Triumphus, Augustinus, 100

Trojans, 89

Tuzet, Hélène, *Le Cosmos et l'Imagination*, 179

Ungaretti, G., 22, 220, 221, 222; *Sentimiento del Tempo*, 221

Urbi et Orbe, traditional papal Christmas greeting, 108

Valeriano, 27

Valla, Lorenzo, 99

Vatican City, 193

Vatican Council I, 197

Vatican Council II, 200

Vedusti, (view-painters), 170

Venus, 87, 91, 92, 93; Temple of Venus and Rome and Cult of *Roma Aeterna*, 92, 93